(with Scripture)

for Busy Grandpas

Richard Frisbie

ACTA Publications

Chicago, Illinois

**For Abigail, Annie Maude, Charles,
Charlotte, Christopher, Clare, Emily,
Lauren, Matthew, Nora, Philip and Timothy**

Daily Meditations (with Scripture) for Busy Grandpas
by Richard Frisbie

Edited by Gregory F. Augustine Pierce
Cover Artwork by Isz
Design and Typesetting by Garrison Publications

Published by ACTA Publications, Assisting Christians To Act, 4848 N. Clark Street, Chicago, IL 60640, 800-397-2282

Library of Congress Catalog number: 98-70833

ISBN: 0-87946-182-9

Printed in the United States of America

02 01 00 99 98 5 4 3 2 1 First Printing

Arks

Amid more animals than Noah had
on the deep,
a first grandchild lies asleep.

The baby is safe under the animals.
They're only stuffed.
And her mother
won't let her smother.

But not all babies come as a gift
    among gifts.
No adoring relatives peek in from
    the hall.
The lone teddy bear faces the wall.

Psalm 10:12-14

*Rise up, Lord God! Raise your arm! Do
not forget the poor! Why should the
wicked scorn God, say in their hearts,
"God doesn't care"? But you do see:
you do observe this misery and sorrow;
you take the matter in hand. To you the
helpless can entrust their cause; you
are the defender of orphans.*

Secret Thoughts

Secret thoughts of first-time grandpas:

At age 50: You're delighted with the baby, of course, but you're not sure you want to be introduced to pretty young women at parties as someone's grandfather.

At age 60: You couldn't help worrying during the mother's pregnancy. You're relieved that she and the baby are both well.

At age 70 and up: Thank God, a grandchild at last.

Psalm 128:6

May you see your children's children.
Peace be upon Israel!

Crimes of the Young

Everywhere you go you see young children misbehaving. In the supermarket, they yammer at their mothers to buy candy. In the library, they lie down on the floor, kicking their feet, and refuse to go home. In church, they bite their big brothers.

In your day, you never allowed that sort of conduct.

A dim memory stirs in the back of your mind. An inner voice says, "Oh, yeah."

Psalm 128:3

Your wife will be like a fruitful vine within your house; your children will be like olive shoots around your table.

Flashback

In the forest preserve a wooden bridge arched a small creek. The children called it the Troll Bridge.

I willingly played the troll while a flock of Billy Goats Gruff trip-trapped across the bridge.

I'd like to play troll for another generation of Billy Goats Gruff and hear once more their laughter, but over the years vandals have burned the bridge.

Who'd have thought there were real trolls in the world?

Psalm 119:95

The wicked lie in wait to destroy me,
but I consider your decrees.

An Orderly Basement

Now that the kids are gone, it's finally time to clean out the basement.

Pack away the old wooden blocks that were kept to prop things up. Get rid of the Ping Pong table that's always been so much in the way.

But what's this? Suddenly there are grand-children rummaging in the boxes and getting things out again.

Maybe basements are no more meant to be orderly than life itself.

Nehemiah 5:5

Now our flesh is the same as that of our kindred; our children are the same as their children.

Grandma

Warm beside me in our bed,

a long winter night ahead.

Not granted for taking,

nor taken for granted.

Song of Songs 1:16

Ah, you are beautiful, my beloved, truly lovely. Our couch is green.

Ears

Grandchildren think I look funny in my winter hat, like a Mongolian sheepherder with one of the sheep on his head.

Resolutely acting cool despite the cold, they wouldn't hear me if I told them that being grown up, finally, means doing what's right despite what others might think.

My ears are warmer than theirs.

Psalm 115:6
> *They have ears, but do not hear; noses, but do not smell.*

Alliances

It's an old joke: grandparents and grandchildren are supposed to get along so well because they share a mutual enemy.

But in the real world the grandparents' sympathy swings from their grandchildren to their grown children and back, depending on who's giving whom a hard time at the moment.

For grandpas, when aid and comfort are needed, there are no enemies.

Isaiah 40:1

Comfort, O comfort my people, says your God.

Toot, Toot

Observing how seldom whistle-blowers in government or industry get anything but grief for their integrity, one is reminded of the early Christian martyrs.

Tradition depicts them standing up to lions.

Grandpas usually try to avoid painful situations. But it's good to know that there are still people whose inner selves are beyond the reach of predators.

Daniel 6:22

"My God sent his angel and shut the lions' mouths so that they would not hurt me, because I was found blameless before him; and also before you, O king, I have done no wrong."

Destinations

The trodden trail has thawed and frozen, thawed and frozen. If he slipped on the ice here, they might not find him before nightfall.

So he follows rougher trails tunneled through the brush by deer. The footing is crunchy enough, but branches stinging his face remind him to stoop to the height of animals only four feet tall.

He thinks of short people he knows, his grandchildren, beginning to wind their ways to uncertain destinations. May they take roads less traveled...and remember to keep their heads down!

---

2 Samuel 22:33-34

The God who has girded me with strength has opened wide my path. He made my feet like the feet of deer, and set me secure on the heights.

Tracks

When your tracks in the snow of life melt at winter's end, who will remember that you passed this way?

Half a century hence, perhaps, someone will recall in casual conversation, "When I was a child, my grandfather used to take me to the woods in the winter and show me where the deer danced."

---

1 Samuel 2:9

"He will guard the feet of his faithful ones, but the wicked shall be cut off in darkness; for not by might does one prevail."

Youth

A father was so distressed that his son wasn't listening to good advice that he wrote him a letter: "You should take care to weigh my words, and you might find my teaching useful; give ear to hear instruction so as to build on long experience; should I allow you to ignore it altogether, you will shoot up a useless weed."

The grandfather of this wayward young man might have said something comforting to the father about never giving up on the young. We'll never know. According to the date of the manuscript, they all lived about 1200 B.C. in a village near Thebes in ancient Egypt.

Job 14:7-9

For a tree there is hope, if it be cut down, that it will sprout again and that its tender shoots will not cease. Even though its root grow old in the earth, and its stump die in the dust, yet at the first whiff of water it may flourish again and put forth branches like a young plant.

Color Me Blue

Researchers say children reveal in their drawings their relationship with their grandparents. When grandparents are part of their lives, kids draw active figures dominating the page, with individualized details.

Grandparents seen only occasionally turn up small and inert, perhaps on the left side of the page. Completely absent grandparents are not present at all in children's imaginations. Asked to draw a grandparent, these children fall back on an image from cartoons or TV.

Only five percent of the children studied had at least one intimate grandparent.

Colossians 3:9-10

Do not lie to one another, seeing that you have stripped off the old self with its practices and have clothed yourselves with the new self, which is being renewed in knowledge according to the image of its creator.

View on a Clear Night

The ancients in their desert stared upward into the clear night and, beyond the stars, dimly glimpsed the face of God.

Modern people go out into our desert not to pray but to plant trees and grass to make it look like Ohio, beclouding the air with humidity and neon lights, and obscuring most of the galaxies.

Where now the face of God?

Isaiah 40:3

A voice cries out: "In the wilderness prepare the way of the Lord, make straight in the desert a highway for our God."

Surprises

Mihaly Csikzentmihalyi, the University of Chicago guru of "flow" and "creativity," says we should all try to be surprised by something every day. That's part of the charm of young grandchildren—they sparkle with surprise at almost everything.

But how can I be surprised when I usually know what's going to happen next? Politicians will not keep their campaign promises. The job that had to be rushed to meet a deadline will, in the end, have to be done over because it was rushed. The grandchild supposed to smile for a family portrait will instead stick out his tongue.

There are some advantages to being almost able to foretell the future. The trick is to remember that pleasant surprises are still possible.

Psalm 37:4

Take delight in the LORD, and he will give you the desires of your heart.

A Passover

One night while he was asleep, he changed from being too young to be promoted to being too old to be promoted.

Or maybe it was that he believed his wife and children needed his presence as well as his pay.

And that what was good for the company wasn't necessarily good for the country...and his family.

He won't be promoted, but he has chosen the better part.

Exodus 12:11
It is the passover of the LORD.

Reprieve

Since the last time he hiked these woods, some-one has violated the verge with a new hotel.

Grandchildren, he thinks, will no longer be able to watch the deer congregate here along the river.

But, as he pauses to enjoy the view of a tributary creek, black against the snow, he sees a deer staring at him after all.

Psalm 104:31

May the glory of the LORD endure forever; may the LORD rejoice in his works.

An Award

The office building won an architectural award. When the grandfather with a briefcase on a luggage carrier enters, however, there's no elevator conveniently close, only an escalator with a sign: NO WHEELED CARTS.

Irritated, the man goes up the escalator anyway. At the top, a guard starts to scold him. The man ignores him and walks on. Why let this petty tyrant spoil his day?

Later he thinks he should have said something pleasant to the guard. Why spoil *his* day? Does anyone ever give *him* an award?

John 13:14-15

"So if I, your Lord and Teacher, have washed your feet, you also ought to wash one another's feet."

Sunday Morning

People say they don't need to go to church because they can find God in a majestic forest.

Yes, God is there, too.

But I would miss the children poking their little siblings, the old neighbors who have knelt beside us for a generation, the men and women who make the church a community.

I don't get much feedback from fallen leaves.

Exodus 20:4

You shall not make for yourself an idol, whether in the form of anything that is in heaven above, or that is on the earth beneath, or that is in the water under the earth.

For Goodness' Sake

A writer and a photographer created a children's version of an exhibit honoring more than one hundred unsung heroes from ten countries who helped save Jews from the Nazis during World War II.

One of the sponsors said, "Kids are very comfortable with evil. They see it every day. But they have a much tougher time studying goodness."

Titus 1:7-8

For a bishop, as God's steward, must be blameless; he must not be arrogant or quick-tempered or addicted to wine or violent or greedy for gain; but he must be hospitable, a lover of goodness, prudent, upright, devout, and self-controlled.

Stuff

There's a difference between familiar, dear possessions and Stuff.

Great-grandmother's mandolin is more than an oddly shaped wooden box with strings. It hums all the old songs even when no one is playing it.

But it is Stuff—the excess of an affluent age—that crowds the closets.

If we don't get rid of most of it soon, whatever will the children do with it?

Genesis 45:20

*"Give no thought to your possessions,
for the best of all the land of Egypt is
yours."*

Grandchildren Far Away

An oak tree grew on a sunny bank as a sapling.

The years passed. The creek eroded the bank and undermined its roots.

Half of the roots, still buried in soil, cling to life. The other half clutch futilely at the air over an abyss.

In its days of glory, the tree cast a broad shade and dropped acorns into the stream to race away to far places with each freshet.

Now the young trees have jobs and families in New York and Dallas and San Diego.

Ezekiel 17:23

Under it every kind of bird will live; in the shade of its branches will nest winged creatures of every kind.

Hard Question

What were you thinking, Lord,
to let this happen to a child
asleep in her bed?

A bullet through the wall
fired by a stranger.

You know how hard her mother
tried to give her a better life
than she herself had known.

Even here in the shadow of your steeple
bad things happen to the best of people.

Job 5:7

*Human beings are born to trouble just
as sparks fly upward.*

Dilemmas

In a moderately repressive country, police arrest two members of the political opposition. In separate cells, each is asked to accuse the other. The one who agrees first will be released at once. The other will be locked up indefinitely.

If both are weak, both stay in jail. If both are strong, the police will let them go.

In real life, the pressures usually aren't that dramatic. But life does teach that doing what's right makes us free in the long run.

John 8:36

"So if the Son makes you free, you will be free indeed."

Winter

About now, it seems that winter has been going on since cars had rumble seats.

Suggestion: invite the youngest grandchildren to spend Sunday afternoon at your house playing with something messy while their parents see a movie.

Fingerpaints, maybe. Anything messy is always a hit.

When their mommy takes them home for their naps, see if spring doesn't seem closer than you thought.

Mark 13:18-19

"Pray that it may not be in winter. For in those days there will be suffering, such as has not been from the beginning of the creation that God created until now, no, and never will be."

Archangels

On an expedition to show them their heritage, the little boys gawked at the statue on the facade of St. Michael's Church. Their suburban church, attractive in its way, lacks the old-time craftsmanship and splendor that immigrants financed with their dimes.

A grandpa sometimes forgets the outlook of little kids. They pay no attention to his explanation of the symbolic roles of angels. They ask why St. Michael grasps a stone sword as long as a canoe.

"To whack the bad angels with," he says. They like that answer much better.

Matthew 24:31

"And he will send out his angels with a loud trumpet call, and they will gather his elect from the four winds, from one end of heaven to the other."

Telling Stories

As we get older, we like to reminisce about the past. That's sometimes a mistake. It confirms younger people in their view of us as old fogies.

But grandchildren need to know the family history. They even may be *interested* in our stories about the old days. That's another of the delights of having grandchildren.

Genesis 12:2

"I will make of you a great nation, and I will bless you, and make your name great."

Discipline

Ogg, the cave grandfather, thought the cave grandchildren needed more discipline.

They threw rocks at the tame wolf and failed to belch politely after their aurochs-tail soup, as cave etiquette required.

So it has been ever since.

But it isn't help with discipline that young families need. It's help with giving each child enough attention.

Colossians 3:21

Fathers, do not provoke your children, or they may lose heart.

Heritage

In a newspaper interview, a young woman in California told the story of a gold ring she always wears. It came to her from her grandfather who owned a business in Holland during World War II. It was given to him in gratitude by a business contact, a Jew.

When the Nazis began rounding up Dutch Jews, the grandfather hid his Jewish friend in his warehouse for many months. Then the worst seemed to be over, and the friend thought it was safe to leave. The grandfather grieved the rest of his life that his friend came out too soon and fell into the hands of the Nazis after all.

The woman looks at the ring every day and remembers her grandfather's example. When she someday has children, she will tell them of their honorable heritage.

Psalm 71:21

You will increase my honor, and comfort me once again.

Aliens

Why do there always have to be lepers?

If we don't have real lepers, we invent them. The latest recipients of this unwanted honor are immigrants.

Someday, grandchildren will read about these times and be embarrassed by them.

Then it will be good to be remembered as the grandpa who didn't join the mindless mob.

_____

Leviticus 19:33-34

When an alien resides with you in your land, you shall not oppress the alien. The alien who resides with you shall be to you as the citizen among you; you shall love the alien as yourself, for you were aliens in the land of Egypt: I am the LORD your God.

Eaveslifting

With a lifetime of experience in being sly when necessary, any grandfather ought to be able to contrive from time to time to be "accidentally" overheard saying something nice about a grandchild.

Thinking of what to say shouldn't be hard. Grandchildren *are* wonderful, aren't they?

Psalm 34:11

Come, O children, listen to me; I will teach you the fear of the LORD.

Erratum

In church, I hear hymns in English, more or less, with dangling participles.

In the secular concert hall, I hear Stravinsky's *Symphony of Psalms,* with the chorus singing majestic Latin.

I suppose I am an old fossil or a snob to resist the new church music.

But I am right to refuse to sing dangling participles.

"Omnis spiritus laudet Dominum."

Psalm 150:6

Let everything that breathes praise the LORD!

February Thaw

Astronomers learned centuries ago that the sun shines all the time.

One doesn't think of that in the dark and cold of winter.

Then some bright day in February, the sun focuses its warmth on sheltered places, with a promise of more warmth to come.

Sunshine is like love. It's around all the time, even if one sometimes forgets.

Psalm 26:3

For your steadfast love is before my eyes, and I walk in faithfulness to you.

Applause

Grandpas were created to sit through long school programs and applaud young actors and musicians and dancers.

Grandpas are an especially good audience. They'll clap in all the right places. They won't write mean reviews for the morning papers.

Psalm 9:8

He judges the world with righteousness; he judges the peoples with equity.

Commitment

World War II in the barracks. I'm trying to sleep. Guys are talking after Lights Out about their sexual conquests (ninety percent fictional, no doubt).

What if I had been able to say, "In the future, women will imagine they are freer if you don't marry them. You can move into a woman's apartment—no commitment required. If she nags you about coming home late or buying a motorcycle, you can move out."

I think some of the more insensitive clods would have said, "Hey, I hope I live long enough."

I am pondering how to explain all this to my granddaughters.

Genesis 31:50

"If you ill-treat my daughters, or if you take wives in addition to my daughters, though no one else is with us, remember that God is witness between you and me."

Haunted Houses

Many Native American tribes believed that every dwelling has a spirit. When they entered a dwelling, they tried to get on the good side of that spirit.

I glimpse their thinking when I find myself in a house with white carpeting. I know the spirit of that house disapproves of me because I am a slob. If I weren't a slob, I would like white carpeting.

A house where grandchildren come should have a spirit that does not mind if something gets spilled once in a while.

Leviticus 14:45

He shall have the house torn down, its stones and timber and all the plaster of the house, and taken outside the city to an unclean place.

Rewards of Ritual

The local newspaper reported that some fifth-grade boys were caught sneaking into their school on Sunday afternoon when the building was closed.

Adolescent breaking away seems to be setting in at younger ages these days, when kids have even less judgment and resistance to peer pressure than they would have had a few years ago.

One boy, who ordinarily would have been hanging around with those trouble-makers, missed it all because he had to go to a family dinner at his grandparents' house.

Ephesians 6:12

For our struggle is not against enemies of blood and flesh, but against the rulers, against the authorities, against the cosmic powers of this present darkness, against the spiritual forces of evil in the heavenly places.

No Sale

A local community church grew prodigiously after the church leaders took market surveys.

It might be good to attract so many people, mainly young people, to religion. They might otherwise be wandering in a spiritual desert. Yet, thinking of my grandchildren, I am troubled.

Paul Westermeyer, a church historian, explains: "Christianity is not about selling anything....When we are controlled by the culture around us, our first instinct is to ask about numbers and demographics and polls and how something will play in Peoria. All those things are interesting and important. If we are wise, we will study them and understand them. But we will not be controlled by them. We will be controlled by God's promise to sustain us."

Psalm 119:116

Uphold me according to your promise,
that I may live, and let me not be put to
shame in my hope.

Sour Note

A century ago, a Lutheran churchman commented, "The experience of the centuries has proven that music having an easy and delightful swing and well-sugared is the kind that people will love most readily and afterward loathe most heartily."

Psalm 108:2

Awake, O harp and lyre! I will awake the dawn.

Lunch Crunch

A survey shows that thirty-nine percent of Americans nibble on the job instead of taking a lunch break.

Some observers say people are skimping on lunch to get more time for their personal lives. Others say people are just responding to workloads that require them to keep working with one hand while they eat with the other.

For those occupations that had a tradition of sit-down lunches, the decline of a social meal with friends to break up the work day is a loss.

Ecclesiastes 4:7-8

> *Again, I saw vanity under the sun: the case of solitary individuals, without sons or brothers; yet there is no end to all their toil, and their eyes are never satisfied with riches. "For whom am I toiling," they ask, "and depriving myself of pleasure?" This also is vanity and an unhappy business.*

Learners

He attended a grammar school class reunion. There had been other widely spaced reunions over half a century, but he had not noticed until now that people really can learn something from life.

Shy and quiet eighth graders now talked enthusiastically about their interesting careers. Somewhat catty girls had turned into warm and loving grandmothers. Boys whose sole interests seemed athletic not only had shown leadership in business but were now raising funds for worthy causes.

He knew them all when they hadn't necessarily washed their necks.

---

2 Timothy 3:14

As for you, continue in what you have learned and firmly believed, knowing from whom you learned it.

Family

Just before she died, at age sixty, they laid her great-granddaughter in her arms. She clung to life until she could see the new baby, then let go.

She had lived long enough to experience the redemptive force that can animate a family. Both she and her daughter had been married much too young—to losers.

But she had a second husband who slept night after night in a chair beside her bed while she was sick. And her daughter and the daughter's second husband cheerfully turned their living room into a hospice where she spent her last days with her sense of humor and dignity intact.

Perhaps, when the new great-granddaughter is ready to marry, she will get it right the first time.

Psalm 133:1

How very good and pleasant it is when kindred live together in unity!

Spies

Children are as ubiquitous as termites. That's why grandparents never allow themselves even to think negative thoughts about a grandchild.

If a grandpa says of a grandchild, "he would be so good-looking with a smaller nose" or "it's too bad she isn't doing better in school," that child is certain to be listening behind the sofa.

Genesis 29:17
Leah's eyes were lovely, and Rachel was graceful and beautiful.

Dessert

When a grandchild gets old enough to behave in a restaurant and feel comfortable away from Mommy and Daddy, my wife and I invite him or her out to dinner.

Children bask in the focused attention of two grandparents like young plants in sunlight. They often talk so much they scarcely find time to eat, although they somehow manage to deal with dessert.

They know we won't snitch to their parents about what they ate or didn't eat.

However, we don't go so far as one grandmother who always urged her grandchildren to eat the dessert first so they'd be sure to have room for it.

John 7:37

On the last day of the festival, the great day, while Jesus was standing there, he cried out, "Let anyone who is thirsty come to me"

Scientific Faith

When grandfathers indicate disapproval of some modern trend, younger people may mutter that the aged relative isn't keeping up with the times. It is heartening, therefore, to read of new University of Georgia research that repeated a 1916 survey of scientists. Now, as then, about forty percent of biologists, physicians and mathematicians believe in God. No change in all these years.

And these scientists believe not in some vague Supreme Being but in a God who communicates with humankind and to whom one may pray "in expectation of receiving an answer."

Psalm 32:10

Many are the torments of the wicked,
but steadfast love surrounds those who
trust in the LORD.

Trust

Grandfatherly wisdom: never buy assorted choco-
lates. Grandchildren may come to visit.

What if one of them bites into a chocolate
filled with yucky jelly? Many years later they'll be
telling their psychiatrist that what they learned
from Grandpa was never to trust anybody.

Psalm 33:21
*Our heart is glad in him, because we
trust in his holy name.*

===
Tip
===

Grandchildren often start out with jobs that pay partly in tips. One benefit is learning that a friendly customer who leaves a generous tip can make a long shift seem shorter for a server.

Galatians 5:22

By contrast, the fruit of the Spirit is love, joy, peace, patience, kindness, generosity, faithfulness.

Second Chances

Kids get discouraged when they don't make the team or when they don't get a good part in the school play. That's when they need Grandpa to tell them about people like George Abbott.

He was more than a hundred years old when he was asked to update *Damn Yankees,* a popular musical he had originally created some forty years before. Once again he helped light up a Broadway theater with a hit show.

Hebrews 12:1

Therefore, since we are surrounded by so great a cloud of witnesses, let us also lay aside every weight and the sin that clings so closely, and let us run with perseverance the race that is set before us.

$$\overline{\overline{ZT^2}}$$

Zero tolerance, they say,

for practically anything you can mention.

Zero tolerance, they say,

for normally boisterous teens.

Zero tolerance, I say,

for grownups who can't remember

they once were teens themselves.

John 8:7

*When they kept on questioning him, he
straightened up and said to them, "Let
anyone among you who is without sin
be the first to throw a stone."*

Bumper Sticker

When a grandfather has to drive grandchildren to school, the car *is* a school: driving school.

Ecclesiastes 9:13

> *I have also seen this example of wisdom under the sun, and it seemed great to me.*

Civics Lesson

Why don't our grandchildren say to politicians, "I'll be old enough to vote in two years, and I'll remember that you voted for an unreasonable curfew for young people"?

———————————————

Psalm 137:8

O daughter Babylon, you devastator!
Happy shall they be who pay you back
what you have done to us!

Down, Spot

Grandparents like to look at grandchildren and try to imagine what they'll be like as grownups, when we won't be here to see them.

One thing we can be sure of: they won't have four feet and furry ears.

So why bark at them now?

Deuteronomy 8:5

Know then in your heart that as a parent disciplines a child so the LORD your God disciplines you.

Story Time

When grandchildren get wiggly in a restaurant, it may be a good time for Grandpa to tell a story, perhaps something about St. Francis and an animal.

Children see too many TV cartoons about action heroes butting their way through walls with their heads. St. Francis comforting a sick koala bear who ate too many eucalyptus leaves at a birthday party provides a gentler image.

---

1 John 3:18

Little children, let us love, not in word or speech, but in truth and action.

Babysitter's Reward

For thirty years, Frank McCourt tried to write the story of his tragic childhood in Ireland. As a popular English teacher, raconteur and pal of many prominent New York writers, he could tell that his attempts always had the wrong tone.

Then he had occasion to spend a lot of time looking after his four-year-old granddaughter, Chiara. Listening to Chiara, he observed that children are pragmatic, not emotional. They use language economically, and they tell the truth.

So he started over, trying to tell his story in the voice of a child. His book, *Angela's Ashes,* funny as well as sad, soared to the top of the best-seller lists and won him a Pulitzer Prize.

Psalm 119:160
> *The sum of your word is truth; and*
> *every one of your righteous ordinances*
> *endures forever.*

Perspective

Neil Simon, the author of many Broadway hits, admits that much of his comic material is based on events in his own life. *Barefoot in the Park* wasn't funny when it happened, he has said. Only later did it rearrange itself into a comedy.

One advantage of having lived long enough to be a grandfather is that many events once regarded as major crises have shrunk into mere funny stories.

Psalm 4:8

> *I will both lie down and sleep in peace; for you alone, Lord, make me lie down in safety.*

Wisdom

Marcus Aurelius was a philosopher as well as a capable Roman Emperor. His book of meditations is still studied in Great Books classes.

So it's significant that he starts out in the first line by saying, "From my grandfather Verus I learned good morals and the government of my temper."

Psalm 90:12

So teach us to count our days that we may gain a wise heart.

Pillars

The sports columnists this morning were carrying on about highly paid professional athletes who say their job is to play ball, not serve as role models for youth.

There's some justice in what they say. Why pick on sports figures more than entertainers or politicians?

But aren't we all role models—not just for young people, but for each other?

Psalm 144:12

May our sons in their youth be like plants full grown, our daughters like corner pillars, cut for the building of a palace.

Up a Tree

Somehow it wasn't too scary when a son or daughter climbed a tree. But to see a grandchild in a tree is to want to call the fire department and tell them to bring their helicopter.

Grandpas are good at worrying because we have had so much practice.

Zechariah 9:16

On that day the LORD their God will save them for they are the flock of his people; for like the jewels of a crown they shall shine on his land.

Quality Control

Grandparents like to think someday they'll see their grandchildren graduate *summa cum laude* after having led their team to a championship season.

Meanwhile, they're getting "B" in math, dropping as many fly balls as they catch, and today their socks don't match.

Years ago, people might have said, "That child needs a good talking to."

More likely, what he or she needs is a good listening to. And a grandfatherly hug.

---

1 Thessalonians 5:11

Therefore encourage one another and build up each other.

Leap Day

In order to make the calendar come out even, an extra day is added to February every four years.

Leap Day comes about often enough to set it aside for doing something truly hard—like making up with someone with whom one hasn't been on speaking terms.

Once every four years, that should be manageable.

Colossians 3:13

*Bear with one another and, if anyone
has a complaint against another,
forgive each other; just as the Lord has
forgiven you, so you also must forgive.*

Heroes

A firefighter snatches an old woman from a burning house. Non-professional passersby brave a frigid flood to save a child.

Poorly educated editors keep writing "heroics" in headlines to describe such deeds when they mean "heroism." The good news is that they have many occasions to fall into this error.

Although popular culture for many years has held up "do your own thing" as the new Golden Rule, there are still people demonstrating every day that it is possible to overcome the basic selfishness of the human animal.

Philippians 2:4

Let each of you look not to your own interests, but to the interests of others.

Out of Bounds

A sign is posted at all the entrances to Bloomington, Illinois, that says *Not in Our Town—No Racism*. Putting up a sign doesn't necessarily make it so, but it's not a bad thing to establish a climate that declares racism out of bounds.

Matthew 5:6

"Blessed are those who hunger and thirst for righteousness, for they will be filled."

Summer Bird

She saw herself amid cathedrals and castles, a semi-starving student. The Louvre and Florence would make the sacrifices worthwhile.

But she was the last child at home with her widowed mother. Would it be selfish for her to go to Europe for a whole summer?

She needed a grandfather to point out the obvious. "Your mother has an interesting job and warm friends and neighbors. You have your own life to lead. Go. But write often."

Genesis 1:31

God saw everything that he had made, and indeed, it was very good.

Hard Chairs

Now comes the season of recitals,

first communions, graduations.

Sitting in a hard chair.

Earning a soft spot in grandchildren's hearts.

Showing that we care.

---

1 Corinthians 13:7

(Love) bears all things, believes all things, hopes all things, endures all things.

New Growth

Planted years ago, these trees long shaded the back of the house. Now they are clutching at the roof and pushing against the garage wall.

They will have to be cut down.

The tree surgeon says new trees will spring up, now that they're not overshadowed.

Isn't this the way life's supposed to be? The saplings are like grandchildren.

Colossians 1:11-12

May you be made strong with all the strength that comes from his glorious power, and may you be prepared to endure everything with patience, while joyfully giving thanks to the Father, who has enabled you to share in the inheritance of the saints in the light.

Generosity

A small girl was entertaining younger cousins in her room. She was overheard saying, "It's OK to play with my doll trunk, but don't lock it because sometimes it gets stuck."

She not only was willing to share her toys, she trusted her little cousins to be responsible.

Matthew 6:19

"Do not store up for yourselves treasures on earth, where moth and rust consume and where thieves break in and steal."

Street Scene

A demonstrator amplifying his protest with a microphone directed, with a negative comment, the attention of his hearers to a passerby who seemed uninterested in the Cause.

The passerby indeed was more interested in keeping a luncheon appointment than in the group, which seemed to be blaming Queen Elizabeth II for the ills of modern times.

The passerby resisted the impulse to respond vigorously to the affront. He thought of his grandchildren. He wouldn't have wanted them to see him contributing to the incivility of the age.

He contented himself with reflecting that Queen Elizabeth, whatever her faults, would be unlikely to shout imprecations at a stranger on the sidewalk.

Matthew 5:9

"Blessed are the peacemakers, for they will be called children of God."

The Golf-Course Gosling

Canada geese live many years, and the old grand-father gander was still around to show the goslings many things they ought to know.

How to find the way in fog and darkness by listening to the rest of the flock.

How to adapt to a changing environment.

How to duck when the human grandfathers slice their golf balls into the rough beyond the water hole.

James 1:5

If any of you is lacking in wisdom, ask God, who gives to all generously and ungrudgingly, and it will be given you.

Confused Samaritan I

Walking along a city street with his grandchildren, a man is accosted by a panhandler asking for "spare change." The man fishes in his pocket and gives the beggar a couple of dollars.

The grandfather is aware that he is teaching his grandchildren a lesson.

(But before you follow his example, see the next meditation.)

1 John 3:17

How does God's love abide in anyone who has the world's goods and sees a brother or sister in need and yet refuses help?

Confused Samaritan II

The scene is a city sidewalk. A panhandler is waiting as a grandfather and his grandchildren come out of a restaurant. The grandfather politely declines to make a contribution, and they pass on.

The grandfather explains to the children that experts say the best way to help such people is to support the agencies that work to get people off the street and help them turn their lives around.

(But before you follow his example, see the preceding meditation.)

Acts 20:35

"In all this I have given you an example that by such work we must support the weak, remembering the words of the Lord Jesus, for he himself said, 'It is more blessed to give than to receive.'"

Time

When his grandson was born, Grandpa looked forward to taking the lad fishing someday. Isn't that what grandpas do?

Now that Grandpa is retired, he has the leisure. But the boy lives in another state. Even if he lived closer, his schedule of team sports and music lessons would leave no time for just sitting around on the banks of a creek.

Psalm 48:13

Consider well (the ramparts of Zion);
go through its citadels, that you may
tell the next generation.

Without Arm-Twisting

John Irving, the novelist, once wrote: "I've always admired the rule in wrestling that holds you responsible, if you lift your opponent off the mat, for your opponent's safe return."

If grunting, sweating athletes in the heat of competition can be taught to continue thinking of the other person, maybe it's not too much for grandchildren to be expected to write "thank you" notes.

1 Corinthians 4:24

What would you prefer? Am I to come to you with a stick, or with love in a spirit of gentleness?

Messages

Granddaughter, age two, on the phone, says: "Remember me?"

Children pick up phrases they hear adults use and try them out until they get the context right. It wasn't likely that her doting Grandpa would forget her in the two days since they had been together.

A sadder message was picked up by a family-life researcher. A little girl told her grandmother on the phone: "Don't have time to talk to you now."

Psalm 107:9

For (the Lord) satisfies the thirsty, and the hungry he fills with good things.

Home Work

When a University of California sociologist studied a large company noted for "family friendly" policies, she was surprised that many employees, both men and women, choose to spend more time at work than might be necessary. They seem to find work life more rewarding than family life.

What happens to their kids? The children seemed to be doing well in school and on the playground. But the sociologist wondered, "What if they grow up to be bright and successful and replay the same time-starved life that was taught to them?"

Matthew 6:27

"Can any of you by worrying add a single hour to your span of life?"

Reclamation

When a young person starts being kept after school, talking back to parents and slamming doors, it's time for grandparents to plan an especially nice expedition with just that child.

Extra attention can't hurt.

Luke 15:22-23

> *"But the father said to his slaves, 'Quickly, bring out a robe—the best one—and put it on him; put a ring on his finger and sandals on his feet. And get the fatted calf and kill it, and let us eat and celebrate.'"*

Getting Over Bumps in the Road

A little girl trying a sidewalk bike for the first time is stalled by a bump in the sidewalk. A cousin only about three years older runs to her and says, "I'll help you over the bump. Don't be afraid of falling over. I'll hold onto the handle bars."

Honors in school, sports trophies, modeling contracts or whatever are all very good. What really warms a grandpa's heart is seeing his grandchildren be kind to each other.

It suggests that maybe the grandfather did something right with his own children.

Joshua 2:12

> *"Now then, since I have dealt kindly with you, swear to me by the L*ORD *that you in turn will deal kindly with my family."*

Technocrats

A favorite cartoon theme is the older person flustered by a computer or a VCR. A young child walks up and sets it right. The stereotype is that only the younger generation is technologically savvy.

Question: Wasn't it the generation that's now of grandparent age who invented all this stuff in the first place?

Proverbs 13:22

The good leave an inheritance to their children's children.

The Wit of Brevity

When interviewers asked the famous preacher, Billy Graham, to tell the greatest surprise in his life, he answered, "the brevity of it." He was seventy eight at the time.

---

2 Samuel 14:14

We must all die; we are like water spilled on the ground, which cannot be gathered up. But God will not take away a life; he will devise plans so as not to keep an outcast banished forever from his presence.

Too Much Realism

A movie critic objected to an otherwise well-crafted and suspenseful thriller because at the end the "hero" overcomes and kills the villain, who has become helpless. "No one in the audience cheered," he wrote. "I felt a collective wince."

The problem with movies and television isn't that they depict so much violence and sex. Violence and sex, after all, are part of real life. But somehow, directors and audiences no longer share a set of values in which waiting to see whether virtue will triumph is part of the suspense.

In the theater as well as in life, the good guys don't always win here and now. But audiences feel cheated when the good guys act like the bad guys.

Psalm 1:1

Happy are those who do not follow the advice of the wicked, or take the path that sinners tread, or sit in the seat of scoffers.

Freedom from Responsibility?

At the Franklin Delano Roosevelt Memorial in Washington, D.C., four segments represent not only his four terms as President but also the Four Freedoms he espoused: freedom of worship and speech, freedom from want and fear.

Those were the ideals of a generation formed by the Depression and World War II. How is it that generations that grew up in greater prosperity seem to have lowered their sights?

Proverbs 16:8

Better is a little with righteousness than large income with injustice.

Social Diseases

Local officials everywhere have found that ignoring graffiti begets more graffiti, plus vandalism and other kinds of crime.

Incivility is the same, especially rudeness to children. It's catching.

Ephesians 6:4

And, fathers, do not provoke your children to anger, but bring them up in the discipline and instruction of the Lord.

Repentance

In Japan, when a company harms the public with a blunder, the chairman, after profuse apologies, is expected to resign.

One can't resign as a grandfather, even for the crime of forgetting a birthday. Maybe that's why, according to industry sources, one quarter of all toys sold are bought by grandparents.

Psalm 38:18

I confess my iniquity; I am sorry for my sin.

Tall Stories

Oog, the cave grandfather, rolled a log on the fire and called the cave grandchildren to sit down and hear this story.

There were two hunters. One always brought back his prey to share with the other people. He prospered and killed many deer. The other hunter selfishly kept food for himself. One day, eating all alone, he choked on a bone. Distracted, he didn't notice a crocodile sneaking up. It ate him.

"Myths stretch the mind," says a University of Chicago professor who reads ancient languages like Sanskrit. "They make us realize the alternatives to our ways of thinking of things."

Genesis 7:1

> *Then the LORD said to Noah, "Go into the ark, you and all your household, for I have seen that you alone are righteous before me in this generation."*

Talking

The experts have found that babies grow up smarter if a loving person talks to them a lot.

So you're doing your grandchildren good in more ways than one when you tell them things they need to learn, such as to shun restaurants that serve french fries with everything and to avoid movies that depict more then two major explosions.

Deuteronomy 6:6-7

Keep these words that I am command-ing you today in your heart. Recite them to your children and talk about them when you are at home and when you are away, when you lie down and when you rise.

The Lamp in the Window

Grandpas can remember when almost every picture window framed a lamp. Pundits lamented that America was becoming too homogeneous, with the power of mass marketing overwhelming traditional values rooted in diversity.

Now, segmented marketing sorts potential customers by sex, income, age, race and other variables. Social critics say America is losing its sense of a common culture.

But opinion polls continue to show that, despite all these changes, about the same proportion of Americans cling to their religious faith. In fact, the percentage of Americans who say they went to church last week has risen slightly since the 1930s.

Ephesians 6:10

Be strong in the Lord and in the strength of his power.

Neighbor

The man always spoke kindly to the children on the block. Being retired, he had time to put bicycle chains back onto their sprockets and listen to whatever the children wanted to tell him.

When the word spread that he had become a grandfather, one neighbor boy expressed concern that the man might now have less time for his young friends. His sister, of an age unburdened by such logic, declared joyfully that she still had "three grandpas."

Psalm 97:11

Light dawns for the righteous, and joy for the upright in heart.

Audio Tour

A "for sale" sign in front of a house urges interested persons to arrange for an "audio tour." I suppose it would be like the guided tours in museums that tell you about a painting, then direct you to move on to the other side of the gallery.

I make a note to myself to record an audio tour someday for the grandchildren. "This is the house where your mother lived when she was little and painted on the wall of her room when no one was looking.

"This is the willow tree your father was climbing when he fell out into the park pond during a summer band concert."

Psalm 103:17

But the steadfast love of the LORD is from everlasting to everlasting on those who fear him, and his righteousness to children's children.

Life Happens

In Tolstoy's story, *The Death of Ivan Illich,* a man dying of cancer thinks this can't be happening to him, who was once the little boy "of whom everyone was so fond."

As aging people increasingly observe, bad things happen to everyone sooner or later.

Matthew 11:28

"Come to me, all you that are weary and are carrying heavy burdens, and I will give you rest."

Extended Family

Watching their mother get married again, the two teenagers betrayed no emotion in their expressions. They liked their new stepfather well enough, but they had mixed feelings.

Of course, being teenagers, they had mixed feelings about everything.

The father of the groom, from out of town, stepped up to them at the reception and said, "Well, I guess I'm your Grandpa now." He put out his hand.

After a moment, each of the young people shook it, limply. At least it was a beginning.

---

2 Samuel 16:3

"Today the house of Israel will give me back my grandfather's kingdom."

Solomon

In a California child-custody case, a judge had to decide what to do about a teenage mother who wanted to take her baby and return to Massachusetts to reclaim her scholarship at Harvard University.

The young father's visitation rights would become meaningless. It was a tangled situation with no easy solutions.

In the end the judge decided that the baby would be better off if the mother had a Harvard degree instead of living on welfare in California.

But one of the factors not lightly dismissed by the judge was that the move would separate the baby also from the grandparents.

Psalm 81:11-12

"But my people did not listen to my voice.... So I gave them over to their stubborn hearts."

Hyenas

A little boy remarked one day, "I'm not going to talk to grown-ups anymore. They either laugh at what you say or they don't listen."

Since he was talking to his grandfather at the time, it appears that he didn't think grandfathers counted as grown-ups. Thank God!

Matthew 11:15
"Let anyone with ears listen!"

April Fool

Not usually having to enforce discipline makes grandfathers the perfect butts of April Fool jokes: the ice cube with a fly in it, the vanishing ink blot, the corsage that squirts water in your eye.

In a life dominated by parents, teachers, coaches, scoutmasters, den mothers, crossing guards, park rangers, choir masters—the list goes on—children need to be on top once in a while.

I do draw the line at whoopee cushions.

---

2 Corinthians 11:19

For you gladly put up with fools, being wise yourselves!

Values

As a trustee of a public library, I find myself counseling parents who are upset because their child encounters a book they feel is unsuitable. I explain that a public library is supposed to buy books appealing to diverse tastes.

Then I pull rank as a grandfather. Besides, I tell them, as children grow up they inevitably will have experiences you'd rather spare them. But when something troubling does occur it's a chance to talk about values.

Grandpas also know that when you look back after the kids are grown, you realize that many an apparent crisis proved in the long run not to amount to much after all.

Baruch 3:5

Do not remember the inequities of our ancestors, but in this crisis remember your power and your name.

Grandpa-Aged

Marketers are discovering that the nation is becoming grandpa-aged.

"There are right now seventy million Americans fifty years of age or older with another seventy plus million coming right behind them," proclaims a marketing trade publication, warning marketers away from their current preoccupation with younger audiences.

The problem is that older people are harder to sell things to. Instead of rushing to buy something promoted as trendy, we take that as evidence nobody will want it in a couple of years—especially not us.

Proverbs 23:26
> *My child, give me your heart, and let your eyes observe my ways.*

To the Rescue

In a tale from India by Meena Arora Nayak, a young woman is warned by local astrologers that she has to find a future husband with a horoscope that matches hers or the marriage will kill him.

This scares off one suitable prospect.

The girl is told that if she symbolically marries a pipal tree the tree will die instead and she can safely marry anyone she likes. All that's necessary is for someone to find the right tree. That task falls to her grandfather.

The theology here creates a considerable cultural divide, but I leap it easily to walk with her grandfather as he trudges across the fields in rain and in hot sun to find the tree that will make his granddaughter happy.

Song of Songs 2:7

I adjure you, O daughters of Jerusalem, by the gazelles or the wild does: do not stir up or awaken love until it is ready!

Sad Campers

Seven percent of children at summer camp for the first time stay homesick all week.

A couple of years later, many of the same campers who missed their parents so much can't wait to get out of the house to spend all their waking hours in the teen jungle with their friends.

Fortunately, grandfathers can reassure the parents temporarily abandoned by teenagers that the kids in time will find their way home again.

Matthew 15:14

*"They are blind guides of the blind.
And if one blind person guides another,
both will fall into a pit."*

Commentary

In a competition for stories about grandchildren, the winner was the saga of a four-year-old in California who was told to put two dollars in the collection basket. Instead, he said loudly, "I'm not paying, I'm not paying."

It is not known whether he intended a comment on the length of the liturgy or the quality of the sermon. Even the priest laughed so hard he had to pause a moment to collect himself.

In such a situation, a mere parent would have been embarrassed. A grandfather, knowing the penchant of small children for speaking their minds, would simply be grateful the lad didn't say something more, like, "Why does that guy have those funny clothes on?"

Psalm 15:1-2

> *O LORD, who may abide in your tent?*
> *Who may dwell on your holy hill?*
> *Those who walk blamelessly, and do*
> *what is right, and speak the truth from*
> *their heart.*

Tribal Elders

Maggie Kuhn, founder of the Gray Panthers, once said: "We are the tribal elders. We're concerned about the tribe's survival. Our job is to secure the future for the young."

It's not as easy to be a tribal elder now as it was when a grandfather could sit with other geezers in the shade and pass collective judgment on whether it was time to plant the barley or take the goats to the summer pastures.

Although it's hard to give younger people worthwhile advice on such contemporary concerns as career options or real estate values, we still have a good idea of what's good for our grandchildren. Well, some of us, anyway.

Isaiah 24:23

Then the moon will be abashed, and the sun ashamed; for the LORD of hosts will reign on Mount Zion and in Jerusalem, and before his elders he will manifest his glory.

Rebellion

When children get to be teens, it's hard for them to resist peer pressure to do something they not only know is wrong but don't really want to do anyway.

One excuse they can use, if adopting an anti-parent posture is in vogue among their friends, is "my grandfather will kill me if I do that."

The truth is that, even while rebelling against their parents, kids may very well still care what Grandpa thinks.

---

2 Samuel 22:9

> *Smoke went up from his nostrils, and devouring fire from his mouth; glowing coals flamed forth from him.*

Human Nature

The media have presented innumerable feature stories about how Generation X is "different." Now Generations Y and Z are coming along.

Considering how little human nature has changed in the thousands of years of recorded history, how much can people change in one generation?

Genesis 3:8

They heard the sound of the LORD God walking in the garden at the time of the evening breeze, and the man and his wife hid themselves from the presence of the LORD God among the trees of the garden.

Compassion

Anthropologists found people in Africa some years ago who seemed to have lost their capacity to show compassion, even to other members of their own tribe.

If someone fell and injured himself in circumstances that would ordinarily bring people running to help, the tribesmen would merely laugh.

The explanation was that the tribe had been ground down by generations of disasters and hardship.

What is one to say about waning compassion in a country where most people are better off than at any time in history?

Mark 8:2

> *"I have compassion for the crowd, because they have been with me now for three days and have nothing to eat."*

Custody

Three weeks after retiring to travel, the man and his wife were given custody of their four-month-old grandson because their daughter was mentally ill.

Like other grandparents who unexpectedly have to care for grandchildren, they did their best. Bonding with a small child is rewarding, but as time passed they found chasing a two-year-old full time a considerable drain on their waning energy.

They had more than one reason to rejoice when their daughter showed signs of improving to the point where she could reclaim her son.

John 14:18

"I will not leave you orphaned."

Witnesses

As you enter the grandfather years, you realize

that many of the witnesses to your youthful follies have gone on to better things.

Unfortunately, so have the witnesses to your small triumphs.

Deuteronomy 19:15

A single witness shall not suffice to convict a person of any crime or wrongdoing in connection with any offense that may be committed. Only on the evidence of two or three witnesses shall a charge be sustained.

April 13

Clouds

New research suggests that the contrails left by jet aircraft may widen out to increase the amount of cloud cover over a whole continent.

It is sobering to have to reflect every time we look at the sky how small actions can cast a vast shadow.

Psalm 65:3

*When deeds of iniquity overwhelm us,
you forgive our transgressions.*

Planting a Tree

The Japanese maple I just planted is less than two feet tall, although bearing dense foliage.

It won't amount to much in the time I'll be living in this house, but someday it will flame with glory behind the garage for someone's grandchildren to enjoy.

Planting trees for the future is something grandparents do all the time, even without being aware of it.

Deuteronomy 10:19

You shall also love the stranger, for you were strangers in the land of Egypt.

Grief

A small boy releases a red helium balloon. As it rises, a hot wind carries it off over the rooftops of Oklahoma City.

This is the way he consoles himself for the loss of his grandfather in the rubble of the bombed federal building.

One can imagine the note tied to the string: "I miss you, Grandpa," written as dictated in the neat handwriting of an adult. It is signed with the laboriously printed name of a five-year-old.

John 5:24

"Very truly, I tell you, anyone who hears my word and believes him who sent me has eternal life, and does not come under judgment, but has passed from death to life."

Gatherings

It doesn't seem long ago that one caught up with the cousins at weddings.

Next came baptisms.

Now that we are grandparents, it's confirmations and graduations that assemble the family.

And funerals.

Jeremiah 31:13b

I will turn their mourning into joy, I will comfort them, and give them gladness for sorrow, says the Lord.

Selling the House

Here is the threshold over which he didn't carry his bride, because when they moved in they'd already been married two years and she was carrying a baby and a lamp.

Here is the place where the swing set used to stand. The grass has never completely recovered.

Here are the scrapes on the side of the garage door memorializing the new drivers who always had trouble backing out, turning and listening to the radio at the same time.

How odd that strangers now will roam these holy halls.

Proverbs 24:3-4

By wisdom a house is built, and by understanding it is established; by knowledge the rooms are filled with all precious and pleasant riches.

Staying in the Harbor

A stiff northeast wind flung whitecaps against the breakwater. Wherever there was a crack, spray geysered up and over. In the shelter of the harbor, people sat in their boats, eating lunch and considering whether to venture out.

Few wanted to risk broken battens and torn sails. So only a few of the larger boats put to sea. In effect, without discussion, the majority voted against leaving the harbor.

One of the harder things a grandfather has to do is persuade the younger generation that the majority is sometimes right.

Psalm 107:28-29

Then they cried to the LORD in their trouble, and he brought them out from their distress; he made the storm be still, and the waves of the sea were hushed.

Success

Two black teenagers in Chicago documented, with the help of a public radio producer, life amid the poverty and violence of the South Side over a period of years.

Their broadcasts won numerous awards, and they distilled a hundred of their radio interviews into a book.

As one of the boys finished high school and headed off for college out of state, he said: "If I fail, I'll be letting my mother down, my grandparents, my community. I'm not going to fail."

Job 15:10

*The gray-haired and the aged are on
our side, those older than your father.*

No Lecture

In *The Education of Henry Adams,* the author speaks fondly of both his kindly grandfathers.

When young Henry was about six and refused to go to school, Grandfather John Quincy Adams took him by the hand and brought him there. Far from resenting this treasonable siding with the enemy, the boy respected his grandfather's restraint.

"He had shown no temper, no irritation, no personal feeling, and had made no display of force. Above all, he had held his tongue."

Afterwards, the boy continued to feel free to play in the library and rummage through the former President's desk as usual.

Ecclesiastes 3:1, 7

> *For everything there is a season, and a time for every matter under heaven...a time to keep silence, and a time to speak.*

Memory

As people age, memory becomes less dependable. Experts advise making up fanciful little stories that list things one needs to remember.

For example, a grandpa with a shopping list could tell a story like this:

When a certain bad little boy wouldn't put on his seat belt to go to the store, a dinosaur came along to gobble him up. But the grandfather distracted it with a dozen eggs, squirted toothpaste in its eyes and hit it over the head with a bag of water-softener salt.

---

2 Peter 1:12

Therefore I intend to keep on reminding you of these things, though you know them already and are established in the truth that has come to you.

Fashion Statement

That grandfathers tend to know who they are without needing to bolster their image artificially is mostly good.

But there are occasions when one probably ought to dress up one notch more than one intended for the sake of the grandchildren.

The much-worn favorite sweater, if seen by their friends, could bring on a case of near-terminal embarrassment.

Deuteronomy 8:4

The clothes on your back did not wear out and your feet did not swell these forty years.

Commencement

The graduates smuggled in balloons, blew them up and threw paper at each other during the ceremony. The grandfather was gratified that at least they did not pour beer over each other's heads, as has been known to happen.

Grandparents of the world need to unite! The reward for traveling long distances and sitting still for a long time should be a commencement speaker worth hearing and a dignified ceremony worth observing.

---

1 Timothy 2:1-2

First of all, then, I urge that supplications, prayers, intercessions, and thanksgivings be made for everyone... so that we may lead a quiet and peaceable life in all godliness and dignity.

Sundays in the Park

One of the great original ideas of the Judaeo-Christian tradition, the Sabbath observance made rich and poor equally free of drudgery once a week, refreshed family life and encouraged reflection.

Now Sunday has become a frantic catch-up day for the tasks that piled up during the week.

We did this to ourselves.

Mark 2:27

Then (Jesus) said to them, "The sabbath was made for humankind, and not humankind for the sabbath."

Adventure

Whenever I stand by a river, I feel the urge to launch a canoe and follow the current. I want not only to see what's around the next couple of bends, but to experience the river's course all the way to the ocean.

At my age, it's a symbol of many adventures I finally realize I'll never get around to.

But my grandchildren are growing up. Some of them will go places I have never been. I hope I have helped prepare the way.

Deuteronomy 1:33

"(The Lord) goes before you on the way to seek out a place for you to camp, in fire by night, and in the cloud by day, to show you the route you should take."

The Old Goat

Aunt Tessie said Grandpa was a "disreputable old goat." And it was true that the boy sometimes could smell booze on Grandpa's breath.

The boy found out eventually there was an additional reason his family generally disapproved of the old man: despite his age, he had "girl friends."

But from the boy's point of view, all this was irrelevant. Grandpa took him to the park and to the zoo. Grandpa was as lively as Monkey Island and fun to be with.

Grandpa loved him.

1 Peter 4:8

Above all, maintain constant love for one another, for love covers a multitude of sins.

Spoiling

One set of experts says spoiling the grandchildren is exactly what grandparents are supposed to do. That partly makes up for the regimentation modern children experience from teachers, coaches, playground supervisors, lifeguards, park rangers and other adult authorities.

Other experts say no, grandparents should follow the parents' rules about suitable activities, behavior and food. At a time when standards of conduct have broken down, grandparents should not undermine parental discipline in any way.

Suggested compromise: do whatever daughters and daughters-in-law will let you get away with.

Genesis 31:49

"The Lord watch between you and me, when we are absent one from the other."

Amen, Amen

The boy had an uncle who was much like a grandfather. Only sporadically employed during the Depression, the uncle had time to take the boy to the beach and teach him to swim.

As the boy grew older, he enjoyed hanging around his uncle's college-professor friends and listening to the grown-ups talk.

Decades later, he still remembers standing next to the piano with his uncle/"grandpa" while a music professor worked through the score of Wagner's opera *Parsifal* and explained how it was all based on the way they sang "amen" in Dresden.

A child who doesn't have a real grandfather at hand tends to create one.

Romans 8:15

For you did not receive a spirit of slavery to fall back into fear, but you have received a spirit of adoption.

Joyful Noise

Driving up to a house where grandchildren live, the grandfather sees the children smiling through a window.

They aren't glowering in a corner.

They haven't retreated to a tree in the backyard.

They aren't hiding under their beds.

Instead, they are hopping around the living room shouting, "He's here, he's here."

Psalm 100:1

Make a joyful noise to the LORD, all the earth.

Granddogs

Two large frisky dogs at a family backyard party saw that the gate stood open. As they gamboled out to freedom they met the grandfather in the driveway.

He pointed to the gate and said firmly, "Hey. Get back in there."

To his surprise, they both turned around and obeyed.

They weren't his dogs, but as granddogs they seemed to accept the authority of the patriarch of the family.

Perhaps even in these times a grandfather possesses more influence than he realizes.

Luke 11:33

"No one after lighting a lamp puts it in a cellar, but on the lampstand so that those who enter may see the light."

Quick Study

In many families grandparents are losing their traditional roles as repositories of family culture and history. For some children, "Grandpa" is just a name signed to a birthday card (or check) mailed from a distant city.

That's probably why travel agents report an upswing in the number of grandparents setting up trips with grandchildren. If nothing else, the stresses of travel can bring people closer together, like the survivors of tornados and earthquakes.

Isaiah 57:19

Peace, peace, to the far and the near, says the LORD; and I will heal them.

Abuses

Spurred by all the real child abuse in the nation, authorities and busybodies sometimes overreact.

In a Chicago suburb, a sleeping child was left in a car for a few minutes while his mother ran into a store. When she came out, instead of being advised this wasn't a good idea, she was arrested.

In a New York City park, when a little boy couldn't make it to a distant restroom, his grandmother let him pee in the bushes. She was arrested.

Doesn't anyone stop to think how long it takes a small child to get over the trauma of seeing a parent or grandparent busted?

Revelation 2:10

Do not fear what you are about to suffer. Beware, the devil is about to throw some of you into prison.

Matching Dresses

The mother and her little daughter turned up wearing matching dresses.

Because the little girl already resembled her mother in personality as well as appearance, the dresses created the illusion that some confused time machine had mixed past and present together.

The grandfather found this curiously satisfying.

Genesis 24:23

"Tell me whose daughter you are."

Toys

When the children grow up and move out, one consolation to their parents is not having toys scattered around the house to be picked up or tripped over.

But when grandchildren appear, wise grandparents reinstall a stock of toys.

Younger grandchildren pitch in and play with them. Older grandchildren, past the age of putting the yellow triangular peg in the yellow triangular hole, look around and at least feel welcome.

They may even say, "Aw, do we have to go home now?"

Matthew 10:13

"If the house is worthy, let your peace come upon it."

Quality Time

Feature articles on parenting are always recommending "quality time" with children.

Fortunately, children often consider time with grandparents to be quality time. That's because we can live with them in the present moment, giving no thought at all to their latest report cards or class standings.

Psalm 69:13

But as for me, my prayer is to you, O LORD. At an acceptable time, O God, in the abundance of your steadfast love, answer me.

"Did I Ever Tell You About the Time...?"

Grandfathers shouldn't hold back from telling stories about family history. That's the advice of experts who study such things.

When older people catch themselves repeating the same stories, they may stop talking about old times entirely for fear of boring the young folks.

But children gain a sense of security from a connection with the past. They come to realize they are not lone individuals in an uncaring world but part of a family with accomplishments and traditions.

---

2 Thessalonians 3:6

Now we command you, beloved, in the name of our Lord Jesus Christ, to keep away from believers who are living in idleness and not according to the tradition that they received from us.

Staying in Touch

A new home for the aged sits in a park-like campus in a quiet neighborhood. Flowers surround new low buildings. Birds sing in the trees.

The new home replaces a graceless brick block on a busy highway. The old folks used to sit out on the high wooden porches on warm days and watch the pickup trucks coming and going at the grain elevator, picking up feed and fertilizer.

That view gave them contact with the real world. The old home wasn't all bad.

Genesis 27:39

"See, away from the fatness of the earth shall your home be."

Progressive Paranoia

Father: If you're going to climb that tree, be sure to hang on.

Grandfather: You'd better come down out of that tree. You might fall.

Father: Say, that *is* a great trick you do on the trapeze.

Grandfather: I can't look.

Father: Stay here a minute. I'll be right back.

Grandfather: Stay here a minute. These two armed guards I've hired will watch you until I get back.

So speaks the same man at different ages.

Psalm 16:1

Protect me, O God, for in you I take refuge.

Taking an Interest

Most grandfathers have a considerable capacity to follow the details of grandchildren's lives: the stubborn earache, the mean teacher and the nice principal (or vice versa), the bad-influence play-mate, the team standings, the favorite books.

With whom else on this planet can his adult children chew over such things and find so much mutual interest and sympathy?

---

2 Samuel 9:7

"Do not be afraid, for I will show you kindness for the sake of your father...."

Solidarity

Grandma's grandfather was a union organizer in the days when the police sometimes shot strikers.

Gangsters tried to kill him. The Klu Klux Klan ran him out of one state.

But in the end he succeeded in organizing unions so that working men and women could earn living wages and a degree of dignity.

That's a good way for a grandfather to be remembered.

---

2 Samuel 9:7

"...I will restore to you all the land of your grandfather."

Offline

In the popular mind, as formed by the media, all young people are computer wizards while people of grandfather age are hopelessly incompetent.

In reality, many grandfathers have the wisdom to use computers as tools that are highly useful for certain tasks, while recognizing other applications as unfruitful time-wasters.

A tool is a tool, not a way of life.

Deuteronomy 27:5

And you shall build an altar there to the LORD your God, an altar of stones on which you have not used an iron tool.

Community

Across the nation, community organizations report declining membership. People say they are too busy to come to evening events.

In the daytime, delivery drivers can't find anyone home in a whole block. Everybody's working.

This is a Zen sort of question: if a community has no people willing to come together, is it really a community?

---

1 Corinthians 1:3

Grace to you and peace from God our Father and the Lord Jesus Christ.

Self-Esteem

The business meeting's loudest quack

merely hides an inner lack.

The hoodlum with his hidden gun,

psychiatrists agree, has none.

But children grow up strong and wise

who see themselves through Grandpa's
  eyes.

---

1 Samuel 16:7

"The LORD does not see as mortals see;
they look on the outward appearance,
but the LORD looks on the heart."

Chips Off the Old Blockhead

From time to time, a grandfather sees a grand-child doing something, for better or for worse, the same way he himself did it at the same age.

Blessed are those who have good memories.

Mark 3:28

"Truly I tell you, people will be forgiven for their sins."

Hugs

Some of the best hugs

come just above the knee.

The hugger's so much shorter

than the old huggee.

Psalm 132:9

Let your faithful shout for joy.

Advice

Grandfathers, who have lived long and seen much, often find only frustration in trying to talk people they love out of doing things that probably will turn out to be big mistakes.

One consolation: even God has the same problem.

Psalm 81:13

O that my people would listen to me,
that Israel would walk in my ways!

Grandpa's Academy

In Victorian times, when boys approached the age of rebelliousness, middle-class families dispatched them to a school like Eton or its American equivalent to learn discipline and manners.

Grandpa's house can still be a place for young people to hang out, and perhaps learn something, when they and their parents can't stand each other one more minute.

James 1:19

You must understand this, my beloved: let everyone be quick to listen, slow to speak, slow to anger.

Grandpa Government

Government should be like unto a good grandfather.

He tries to provide a peaceful environment in which everyone can develop.

He doesn't meddle in anyone's personal life.

If someone is in trouble, he will sometimes write a check.

---

1 Peter 5:3

Do not lord it over those in your charge, but be examples to the flock.

Grandparents-in-Law

At family gatherings, a grandpa is sometimes reminded that the other grandparents claim exactly the same biological relationship to a grandchild that he does.

Surely, he thinks, the child looks at least a little bit more like his side of the family.

Of course, the other grandparents are agreeing on their way home that the child looks at least a little bit more like *their* side of the family.

Psalm 37:6

He will make your vindication shine like the light, and the justice of your cause like the noonday.

They Have a Dream

Back in the 1960s, many blacks and whites stood together for an end to segregation. Many of them now are grandparents, whose children and grandchildren don't recall the spirit of those days.

But as long as those grandparents live, the dream of Martin Luther King, Jr., will linger in the world.

Psalm 90:4

For a thousand years in your sight are like yesterday when it is past, or like a watch in the night.

Quick Study

On a family hike in the woods, the two-year-old began singing an old George M. Cohan song, "Every heart beats true, for the red, white and blue...." Both words and melody were recognizable.

"Where did she learn that?" the grandfather asks. Her mother shrugs. Kids today are exposed to so much: television, radio, day care, play groups, babysitters.

The grandfather suddenly remembers the mother at the same age. She too was quick to learn.

Psalm 19:1-2

The heavens are telling the glory of God; and the firmament proclaims his handiwork. Day to day pours forth speech, and night to night declares knowledge.

Labor Saving?

Technological unemployment, which started with hand weavers at the beginning of the Industrial Revolution, has reached middle managers in the Age of the Computer.

But the real victims of technology long have been restless kids, who need challenges to occupy their time. Children used to guard sheep from the wolves or drive mules pulling a farm wagon and feel they had value in the adult world.

Now there's not much to do beyond mowing the grass and taking out the garbage.

Every new labor-saving device paradoxically makes life harder for bored young people, as they are tempted to use their energies in nonproductive ways. This in turn can create stress for grandpas.

Psalm 90:17

Let the favor of the Lord our God be upon us, and prosper for us the work of our hands—O prosper the work of our hands!

Whose Kids Are They?

Waiting for a traffic light on a downtown street, a man says to his friend: "I think kids belong to their parents until they're eighteen." I don't know what he meant. The light changed. Everyone moved on.

Children don't belong to their parents or their schools. Children belong most of all to themselves.

As for ownership of anyone, children own their parents...and their grandparents too.

Romans 8:14

For all who are led by the Spirit of God are children of God.

Critics

Little children are like dogs: they accept grandpas uncritically—wrinkles, warts and all.

Older kids prefer not to be embarrassed in front of their friends by a grandpa wearing an old checked shirt that should be taken with tongs and put out of its misery.

Psalm 31:1

In you, O Lord, I seek refuge; do not let me ever be put to shame; in your righteousness deliver me.

Influence

Grandparents sometimes have more influence than anyone else over troubled teens. Researchers talked to one eighteen-year-old felon who said he never tried to rob old people because they reminded him too much of his grandmother.

"She was the only person who was good to me when I was a kid," he said. "It was when she died that I started getting into trouble."

Psalm 103:13

As a father has compassion for his children, so the LORD has compassion for those who fear him.

Worry

Experts estimate that about half of today's grand-parents will live long enough to become great-grandparents.

So Grandpa may well find himself Great-Grandpa, worrying about the health of the new baby, fretting over the new father's job, and wondering if the new *grandparents* are really saving enough for retirement.

Matthew 6:34

"So do not worry about tomorrow, for tomorrow will bring worries of its own. Today's trouble is enough for today."

Refuge

When Betty Shabazz, widow of Malcolm X, died of burns, her twelve-year-old grandson was accused of setting fire to her apartment because he wanted to go home to his mother.

His grandmother had taken him in because his mother had troubles of her own. Grandma was following the grandparental instinct to stand by their grandchildren no matter what.

That this case turned out tragically should not obscure the millions of times children have taken temporary refuge with Grandma—or Grandpa—to the benefit of all.

Psalm 17:8

Guard me as the apple of the eye; hide me in the shadow of your wings.

Absentee Grandpas

Although grandparents today are healthier and more energetic than ever, they often are not available to their grandchildren. Research by Dr. Arthur Kornhaber shows that only fifteen percent of grandchildren enjoy close grandparents. He deplores what modern life is doing to the grandchildren.

Grandpa is still working. He lives in another state. Grandpa and the child's parents don't get along. Grandpa isn't much interested in spending time with grandchildren. He would rather play golf.

Says Dr. Kornhaber, "Nature has accorded special benefits to youngsters who have a vital connection to at least one grandparent."

Matthew 22:2-3

"The kingdom of heaven may be compared to a king who gave a wedding banquet for his son. He sent his slaves to call those who had been invited to the wedding banquet, but they would not come."

Good News

Back in 1982, public health studies suggested that by 1994 there would be two million Americans over sixty-five seriously disabled. Instead, there turned out to be only eight hundred thousand. One hopes the rest of them are busy taking grandchildren to the zoo.

The experts attribute this to better-educated older people smoking less, exercising more and eating healthier diets.

By 2004, Duke University researchers expect the number of disabled seniors to decrease by another hundred thousand, despite continued increase in the elderly population.

It's a good time for grandchildren to look forward to outings with Grandpa.

Deuteronomy 34:7

Moses was one hundred twenty years old when he died; his sight was unimpaired and his vigor had not abated.

"Cheap Forgiveness"

In making notes for this book, I wrote down a thought I read somewhere: "Beware of cheap forgiveness." When I dug the quote out some weeks later, I couldn't remember what point I was going to make. Isn't a forgiving nature supposed to be good?

Brooding about this, I began to notice grandpas who were perhaps too generous. They held back from expressing an opinion on children's conduct that was truly outrageous. They lent money to relatives who, instead of paying it back, came round for another loan.

People who work with society's losers say there is a fine line between constructive compassion and encouraging dependency.

Matthew 18:32

> *"I forgave you all that debt because you pleaded with me. Should you not have had mercy on your fellow slave, as I had mercy on you?"*

Grandchild Welfare

Patrick T. Murphy, the public guardian of Cook County, Illinois (which includes Chicago), favors a better way to structure child-welfare agencies. He's often in court suing them either for heavy-handed intervention in family life or for failure to act sooner in cases of criminal child abuse.

Murphy suggests splitting child-welfare services into two agencies. One would provide support to help troubled families pull themselves together. The other would move in on the cases in which children genuinely need protection.

It sounds like something a good grandpa would do.

Psalm 35:27

"Great is the LORD, who delights in the welfare of his servant."

Doing Things Right

A granddaughter, hearing plans for a family camping trip, stamps her foot and says, "I'm not going." There will be bugs. And no sending out for pizza. And how will she wash her hair?

They mention that Grandpa is coming along on the trip. She reconsiders. She knows Grandpa can fix holes in mosquito netting. And Grandpa won't forget a can opener as *certain people* did last year.

Hearing the story, Grandpa chuckles. He remembers when her mother could never find her shoes to go to school because they were behind her door.

It's a big responsibility to be looked up to. Grandpa thinks. And it's not enough to do just the little things right.

Ecclesiasticus 37:19

> *A man may be wise and benefit many,*
> *yet be of no use to himself.*

Principles

The Mothering Principle is to make allowances for a child, to bend the rules sometimes so as not to crush a little spirit.

The Fathering Principle is to teach playing by rules. There's a world out there quite ready to trample all over little spirits that haven't learned to adjust.

The Grandfathering Principle is to pretend not to notice anything a child does when parents are present and, when they're not, to intervene only to preserve life, limb and sanity.

Luke 6:37

"Do not judge, and you will not be judged; do not condemn, and you will not be condemned. Forgive, and you will be forgiven."

Fishing

Grandfathers traditionally are supposed to take grandchildren fishing and impart the kind of lifelong wisdom that comes to be quoted in *Readers' Digest*.

I may never earn my Grandfather Merit Badge. Fishing bores me.

I do like messing around in boats. And I do like to take grandchildren with me to help mess around.

I'm hoping that counts.

Matthew 7:9-10

"Is there anyone among you who, if your child asks for bread, will give a stone? Or if the child asks for a fish, will give a snake?"

Caravan

Every morning the march resumes.

The people band together for defense against brigands and to help each other ford foot-numbing streams and climb mountain passes above the clouds.

But as the journey lengthens, first one, then another, can no longer keep up.

Dear friends, even spouses, children and grandchildren, have to be left behind.

And in the morning the caravan marches on.

Psalm 5:3

O LORD, in the morning you hear my voice; in the morning I plead my case to you, and watch.

Bonding

A little girl had been living with her grandmother and aunt. Then the grandmother died, and the aunt decided she couldn't care for the orphan by herself.

So she took her to live with her grandfather in a shack in the mountains, much to the grandfather's surprise. A gruff old hermit, he suddenly had to accommodate his lifestyle to a five-year-old. Today, the authorities surely would have interfered.

But this is the story of Heidi, and that well-loved tale is still popular more than a century after it was first published. The idea that a little girl and her elderly grandfather would bond so well still rings true.

Matthew 28:15

This story is still told...to this day.

Summer

This must be the season of regret for grandparents who left their grandchildren behind to move to a retirement community in the sun.

The winter is past in North Dakota or Minnesota or wherever they came from.

In Florida and southern Arizona, the air conditioning is running full time.

The grandchildren are growing full time too, but their grandparents are no longer part of their everyday lives.

Matthew 24:32

"From the fig tree learn its lesson: as soon as its branch becomes tender and puts forth its leaves, you know that summer is near."

"Everything's Bully"

A tale of two grandfathers. One made it plain from the beginning that he did not approve of his son's choice of a bride. The other grandfather also had reservations about his new daughter-in-law, but he made her feel welcomed into the family like another daughter.

Now that a few years have passed, which one gets to see his grandchildren frequently?

Theodore Roosevelt used to take flocks of little boys camping and sailing. They had to be mature enough to dress themselves and to understand that once the adventure was underway, "everything's bully."

Matthew 12:25

> *He knew what they were thinking and said to them, "Every kingdom divided against itself is laid waste, and no city or house divided against itself will stand."*

So There, Disneyland

A survey of forty-five thousand lower grade children by *The Weekly Reader* showed that their first choice for a family vacation would be a visit to their grandparents.

Psalm 36:7-8

How precious is your steadfast love, O God! All people may take refuge in the shadow of your wings. They feast on the abundance of your house, and you give them drink from the river of your delights.

A Day at the Park

My grandfather was a skilled tool and die maker. He had good jobs all his life, except for a couple of years during the worst of the Depression when manufacturing in the U.S. largely shut down.

Rather than sit around the house all day, taking snuff and eating his favorite Limburger cheese, he used to take me to the park. I was four or five years old. My project one day was to pat a robin. Somehow, the birds kept hopping just beyond my grasp.

I didn't mind. A lifetime later, I remember that particular day with my grandfather as illuminated by a golden sunshine one doesn't see anymore. I've probably lasted longer than any of the tools he made.

Matthew 6:26

Look at the birds of the air; they neither sow nor reap nor gather into barns, and yet your heavenly Father feeds them. Are you not of more value than they?

Comes the Revolution

Not all educational innovations work out well. One wonders about the wisdom of the junior high school, which collects in one building all the local children just reaching the age of rebellion.

Here's another educational reform: when junior high kids get in trouble, let the grandpas work it out. Children generally feel no need to rebel against grandparents. Grandpa isn't a symbol of "oppressive" authority. He's just Grandpa.

---

1 Peter 1:22

Now that you have purified your souls by your obedience to the truth so that you have genuine mutual love, love one another deeply from the heart.

The "Invulnerables"

Robert Coles, Harvard University psychiatrist famed for his studies of children, says even disadvantaged children can overcome learning disabilities, physical handicaps, dysfunctional families and other problems to become happy and successful adults.

What makes the difference is one person who genuinely regards and stands by a child even when there are problems.

He calls children who have such mentors "invulnerable."

This mentoring role is a natural for grandfathers.

Psalm 5:7

But I, through the abundance of your steadfast love, will enter your house, I will bow down toward your holy temple in awe of you.

Joy

Jean-Paul Sartre wrote, "I could make my grandmother go into raptures of joy just by being hungry."

Maybe that's why when he grew up and became a famous philosopher, he would argue that, no matter what the circumstances, an individual always has the option to change something for the better. (Such as by going to Grandma's house for lunch?)

Although his Existentialism acquired a popular image gloomier than it really was, it probably would have been even cheerier if Sartre had had grandchildren of his own to have lunch with.

Proverbs 15:15

All the days of the poor are hard, but a cheerful heart has a continual feast.

Make-Believe

Experts say young children encouraged in make-believe tend to grow up less likely to get into fights and more likely to be smart and articulate.

One grandfather has entertained several grandchildren as they passed through the appropriate age with The Tiger Hunt. An overstuffed chair becomes the howdah on an elephant's back. The elephant paces through a dark jungle, while tropical birds screech overhead.

Everyone freezes to listen for the tiger's growl. Girls tend to be satisfied with the hunt itself. Boys like to shoot the tiger in the corner behind the piano, then skin it. They're too young to understand about endangered species.

Ephesians 3:20

Now to him who by the power at work within us is able to accomplish abundantly far more than all we can ask or imagine.

Missing It

Grandfathers should exercise and keep as fit as possible, but that's not the same as denying the passing of the years.

Betty Friedan, whose writings helped foster the women's rights movement, is now a grandmother. She told a *New York Times* interviewer: "It's a different stage of life, and if you are going to pretend it's youth, you are going to miss ... the surprises, the possibilities, the evolution."

Psalm 71:9

Do not cast me off in the time of old age; do not forsake me when my strength is spent.

Apparitions

Older people tend to become invisible. They're considered washed up, on the banks of the mainstream, lacking power to influence events and having nothing interesting to say about what's going on today.

So it was amusing to be at large parties with my wife the year *her* latest book was spotlighted in the newspapers.

As knowledge of her identity drifted from one conversation cluster to another, she suddenly became visible again, as if beamed down from a starship.

Isaiah 60:22

The least of them shall become a clan, and the smallest one a mighty nation; I am the LORD; in its time I will accomplish it quickly.

Work

I remember the day my grandfather took me after hours to his machine shop, where real men did real work. I was fascinated by the silent machines and the razor-sharp coils of steel that curled around each drill and router.

In my memory, they still shine like brightest silver.

Psalm 77:12
I will meditate on all your work, and muse on your mighty deeds.

The Link

A great-grandfather in his nineties lay dying. For several days, he had focused inward, not responding to questions, not seeming any longer to be aware of his earthly surroundings.

Nevertheless, the relatives thought it would be a good idea to bring in a newborn great-grandchild.

Somehow, it seemed important to everyone that the baby and the old man should be in the same room together for a few moments, even if neither of them could be aware of the other.

To their astonishment, the old man perked up a moment, smiled and said, "That's a fine baby."

Psalm 33:11

> *The counsel of the LORD stands forever, the thoughts of his heart to all generations.*

Taking Stock

Many grandfathers are old enough to remember acts of kindness during the Depression. They learned that even when almost everyone was experiencing hard times people could still be generous.

What have our grandchildren been learning in recent years, when the nation's sense of compassion seems to have dropped even as the stock market rose?

Genesis 41:35-36

"Let them gather all the food of these good years that are coming, and lay up grain under the authority of Pharaoh for food in the cities, and let them keep it. That food shall be a reserve for the land against the seven years of famine that are to befall the land of Egypt, so that the land may not perish through the famine."

Canoe Trip I

The bow of the canoe slices through the water like a can opener. The old man, now paddling in the stern of the canoe and directing its course, not long ago was a boy paddling in the bow while his grandfather steered.

Now there's a new boy wielding the bow paddle. He looks a lot like the man in the stern.

The boy is preparing someday to be the one who sets the course.

Psalm 78:2

I will open my mouth in a parable; I will utter dark sayings from of old, things that we have heard and known, that our ancestors have told us. We will not hide them from their children; we will tell to the coming generation the glorious deeds of the Lord, and his might, and the wonders that he has done.

Canoe Trip II

On the portages, the grandsons shoulder heavy packs of food and equipment.

Making his way over the rocky trail with a light armload of paddles and boat cushions, the grandfather realizes the little boys who used to sit in his lap are suddenly young men.

He wonders where their voyages will take them.

Joel 2:28

Then afterward I will pour out my spirit on all flesh; your sons and your daughters shall prophesy, your old men shall dream dreams, and your young men shall see visions.

Canoe Trip III

This campsite must have been used for centuries by Indians and fur traders. A breezy promontory with a level top for the tents, not too high above the water, would have attracted anyone who passed that way.

Accompanied by sons and grandsons, the grandfather suddenly becomes a respected chief leading the men of the tribe on an expedition to bring back food to the village.

He swings in a hammock while they fish.

Revelation 14:6

Then I saw another angel flying in midheaven, with an eternal gospel to proclaim to those who live on the earth—to every nation and tribe and language and people.

Now and Then

Adolescents live so much in the present moment that they need influences to counter the excess of Nowness.

That's hard for parents to provide, since they are already perceived as fossils who couldn't possibly understand modern young people.

But grandfathers are so incredibly old that they can sometimes get a teenager's attention with a sentence beginning, "When I was a boy...."

Young people are surprised to find out that Grandpa too once worried about being considered "cool," then decided it wasn't really that important.

Ecclesiastes 7:5
It is better to hear the rebuke of the wise than to hear the song of fools.

Peacemakers

"They really don't mind my butting in. Sometimes they back themselves into a corner with their big mouths. Someone has got to bail them out."

That's one grandmother's view of her role as peacemaker in a rather contentious family, as reported to a researcher. Maybe she's fooling herself about how much the children and grandchildren welcome her interventions, but the argument is plausible.

Grandparents who avoid taking sides often can defuse tense situations within a family. They are living symbols of what holds a family together.

Psalm 29:11

> *May the Lord give strength to his people! May the Lord bless his people with peace!*

Respect

In some African communities, grandparents receive a title that translates more or less to "noble."

I like the sound of that. Instead of the Old Geezer, behold the Noble Grandfather.

Psalm 16:3

As for the holy ones in the land, they are the noble, in whom is all my delight.

Honorable Ancestors

In many traditional cultures, grandfathers symbolize an endless chain of ancestors that disappears into the mists of the past. When people contemplate doing something wrong, if Grandfather's disapproval doesn't deter them it at least makes them nervous.

Even in our own society, if Grandpa has a reputation for rectitude it's a bit harder for a young person to do something Grandpa would not approve of.

Mark 11:10

"Blessed is the coming kingdom of our ancestor David! Hosanna in the highest heaven!"

Why They're "Great"

Forty percent of grandparents now live long enough to become great-grandparents.

Just as grandfathers usually don't have to make grandchildren pick up their socks, great-grandfathers are removed even further from child-rearing responsibility.

In fact, say the experts, all a great-grandfather has to do is remain the living symbol of what a family indisputably has in common.

Psalm 71:18

So even to old age and gray hairs, O God, do not forsake me, until I proclaim your might to all the generations to come.

Obedience Training

Mommy and Daddy are away, so it's up to Grandpa to take the little girl to her ballet lesson.

All he has to do is follow her instructions. "Now you take my hand to cross the parking lot." "This is the door we go in." "This is where the mommies wait."

Grandpa realizes his granddaughter feels more secure than he does.

Psalm 56:3
When I am afraid, I put my trust in you.

"Ambition"

I read this somewhere: children should be cherished for what they are, not what you'd like them to be.

Psalm 139:13-15

For it was you who formed my inward parts; you knit me together in my mother's womb. I praise you, for I am fearfully and wonderfully made. Wonderful are your works; that I know very well. My frame was not hidden from you, when I was being made in secret, intricately woven in the depths of the earth.

Context

Just after grandchildren have finished running through the house in packs, grandparents may feel relieved they've all gone home.

But Dr. Arthur Kornhaber, a leading researcher on such matters, estimates that 30 million children are cut off from their grandparents.

He gets that figure by allowing for geographical separations, divorces and assorted family feuds.

Most of those grandparents can only wish grandchildren would run through their houses in packs.

Psalm 144:15

Happy are the people to whom such blessings fall; happy are the people whose God is the LORD.

What's Doing

The new Golden Rule seems to be Do Your Own Thing Before the Others Do Something Unto You.

Maybe that's because young people spend too much time hanging around with other young people. In former times, young people experienced more of the different generations helping each other and cooperating.

Of course, if Grandpa is off doing his own thing all the time, there's not much to be learned from him.

Ezekiel 36:26

A new heart I will give you, and a new spirit I will put within you; and I will remove from your body the heart of stone and give you a heart of flesh.

Changing Times

When snapshots from family gatherings turn out with glitches, a grandfather cuts out heads or figures for a collage, with a background clipped from a magazine. He does this skillfully, so at first glance the pasting doesn't attract attention.

His grandchildren enjoy the fantasy and hang the collages on their refrigerators. These grandchildren live in a trendy neighborhood, where a playmate—the child of Yuppies—passed the refrigerator one day and noticed that her little friends were pictured inhabiting exotic ruins amid strange-looking tropical vegetation.

"I see you've been out of town," was her blasé comment.

Ruth 4:7

Now this was the custom in former times in Israel concerning redeeming and exchanging: to confirm a transaction, the one took off a sandal and gave it to the other; this was the manner of attesting in Israel.

Birdwatching

A big crow flaps away, its tail feathers pecked by a furious fighter. Presently, a small dark bird returns from the fray and darts across the path to perch in a tree.

"Did you see the white band on its tail?" says the grandfather.

"We saw," say the granddaughters.

When I myself have flown, I hope my grandchildren will remember the kingbird, that doughty defender of nests.

Proverbs 31:9

Speak out, judge righteously, defend the rights of the poor and needy.

Moving Experience

The Chinese masters of *feng shui* have a saying: "To change your life, move twenty-seven objects in your house."

The grandchildren have been visiting. More than twenty-seven objects have been moved.

Psalm 13:6

I will sing to the LORD, because he has dealt bountifully with me.

Power

When the Founding Fathers devised a government of checks and balances, they didn't trust anyone to hold more than a modest amount of power, not even themselves.

Parents are given much power over children, so sometimes Grandpa has to step in like the Supreme Court.

If he overdoes it, he'll be impeached.

Acts 1:8

"But you will receive power when the Holy Spirit has come upon you; and you will be my witnesses in Jerusalem, in all Judea and Samaria, and to the ends of the earth."

Circus Act

As the circus performance ends, the small grand-daughter loses sight of her father in the crowd. Grandpa lifts her onto his shoulders so that she towers above the big people.

When she sees Daddy in the distance, waiting next to his car in the parking lot, she is comforted.

Grandpa enjoys standing so tall.

Sirach 24:13-14

"I grew tall like a cedar in Lebanon, and like a cypress in the heights of Hermon. I grew tall like a palm tree in En-gedi, and like rosebushes in Jericho."

Jobs

The world of work is changing, with many familiar blue-collar occupations simply disappearing. Many white-collar jobs entail so much stress and insecurity that employees are afraid to go home to their families instead of working late.

When the grandchildren finish school, what will work be like for them?

Ecclesiastes 5:18

This is what I have seen to be good: it is fitting to eat and drink and find enjoyment in all the toil with which one toils under the sun the few days of the life God gives us; for this is our lot.

Fair Weather

A much-used sail looks bright against blue sky. It seems as white as the puffy clouds that go with the fair weather. A grandson is at the helm.

This will be a good image to remember when summer is gone.

Proverbs 23:18

> *Surely there is a future, and your hope will not be cut off.*

Growing

Watching his grandchildren at play in a park, a grandfather muses. Will they all make good husbands and wives when their time comes? Will they be good parents to their children?

Will they know when to intervene in the squabble over who gets the next turn with the built-in sand scoop and when to let the kids sort it out for themselves?

Psalm 103:13

As a father has compassion for his children, so the LORD has compassion for those who fear him.

Conceit

I never hear anyone use the word "conceited" any more. Have people—just at this particular moment in history—stopped puffing up their view of themselves?

Or is this the downside of the modern view that high self-esteem is so valuable they try to teach it in school?

When everyone is conceited, nobody notices.

Proverbs 3:34

Toward the scorners he is scornful, but to the humble (the Lord) shows favor.

Bugs and Butterflies

It was a nuisance, a generation ago, returning from a long drive, to have to clean the bug-spattered car. Now, after fifteen hundred miles, the car is surprisingly clean.

But that gives me no pleasure.

While bequeathing grandchildren roads with fewer insects to splat their windshields, we are also creating a world without butterflies along the roadsides.

Genesis 1:25

God made the wild animals of the earth of every kind, and the cattle of every kind, and everything that creeps upon the ground of every kind. And God saw that it was good.

"Beep, Beep"

I think it may be harmless for grandchildren to watch TV cartoons in which the Roadrunner humiliates the Coyote in outrageously sadistic ways. Seeing the natural order of power reversed may relieve the feelings of small children, dominated as they are by bigger children as well as adults.

What is alarming is to see movies aimed at adults become popular even though the protagonists are as mean as the Roadrunner. Anyone with moral sensitivity has to feel sorry for the villains and disgusted with the "heros."

Dare we hope that someday the Coyote will catch that nasty bird and enjoy a well-deserved lunch?

Romans 12:19

> *Beloved, never avenge yourselves, but leave room for the wrath of God; for it is written, "Vengeance is mine, I will repay, says the Lord."*

Book Learning

One of the joys of associating with children is reading them stories. They giggle charmingly when the story's funny and cuddle close at the scary parts.

Advice from a grandpa who knows: never read them "cute" books you don't like yourself. A simpering book depresses their literary taste and will drive you out of your mind when they ask you to read it again for the hundreth time.

Psalm 16:11

You show me the path of life. In your presence there is fullness of joy; in your right hand are pleasures forevermore.

Inequality

Touring a historic mansion or European castle that has been turned into a museum, a grandfather easily imagines himself living there in the days of its glory. As the lord of the manor, of course, not one of the servants.

But in truth most of us are descended from people who lived in the outbuildings and took care of pigs or dug turnips. And, unless the trends in our current economy change, most of our descendants are headed for a new era of bowing and scraping before the rich.

Deuteronomy 25:4

You shall not muzzle an ox while it is treading out the grain.

Evil

Elmore Leonard, a highly successful mystery writer, spins tales in which the protagonists tend to be petty crooks and chiselers. But their character flaws seem minor, as the plots unwind, in contrast to the truly wicked people they have to confront.

Few men reach the age of grandfatherhood without accumulating a list of things they wish they hadn't done. But it still possible to stand up against worse evils.

Psalm 26:9-10

Do not sweep me away with sinners,
nor my life with the bloodthirsty, those
in whose hands are evil devices, and
whose right hands are full of bribes.

True Story

In stern Victorian times, an Irish boy of eighteen worked for his father and lived at home. The father put most of the boy's pay aside for his future.

One day the boy had to go to his father to get some of his earnings to pay gambling debts. The enraged father fired him and gave him his choice of a one-way ticket either to America or Australia. The boy flipped a coin.

Years later, after the boy had raised his own family in America, the story came out for the first time when he told it to his grandchild while they were out fishing.

Moral: if fishermen ever tell the truth, it's to their grandchildren.

Psalm 119:43

Do not take the word of truth utterly out of my mouth, for my hope is in your ordinances.

Mongoose and Coyote

In every culture, grandpas tell similar stories.

Coyote Waits is one of a series of popular novels by Tony Hillerman that feature Navajo tribal policemen instead of the usual hard-bitten city cops.

In one scene, in a city off the reservation, the great-aunt of a young Vietnamese man listens while he tells what he knows of a murder. She comments that in Vietnam there is a saying about how evil keeps intruding in human affairs, like a mongoose pouncing on mice.

The Navajo investigator mentions that in Navajo mythology the coyote, not the mongoose, symbolizes the evil that lurks in everyone. "Coyote is always out there waiting."

2 Chronicles 12:14

He did evil, for he did not set his heart to seek the LORD.

Grandpa to the Rescue

Although the number of grandchildren living with grandparents rose forty-four percent from 1980 to 1990, in many places grandparents are ignored by the legal system.

In earlier times, when grandparents often were less healthy and vigorous than now, everyone assumed they would step in to care for grandchildren when needed.

Now, unless they have been legally appointed guardians, they have trouble registering their own grandchildren in school or authorizing medical care.

Isn't it strange that the authorities make difficulties for today's grandparents, who are probably better able to care for their grandchildren than grandparents ever were before?

Psalm 27:5

For he will hide me in his shelter in the day of trouble; he will conceal me under the cover of his tent; he will set me high on a rock.

Cookie Jar Economics

Sam Rutigliano, pro football coach and television sportscaster, was proud of his Italian immigrant grandfather.

He recalls that Grandpa liked to tell the story of the relative who wanted to borrow some money. Grandpa gave it to him and cut short discussions of the payback terms. "Just put it in the cookie jar when you get it," Grandpa said.

The repayment never came. About a year later, the same relative wanted again to borrow money. "No problem," Grandpa said. "Look in the cookie jar where I asked you to put it."

Psalm 37:30

The mouths of the righteous utter wisdom, and their tongues speak justice.

It Never Ends

As a famous anthropologist, Margaret Mead spent her life studying family relationships in various cultures. When she became a grandmother herself, she said, "I felt none of the much trumpeted freedom from responsibility that grandparents are supposed to feel.

"Actually, it seems to me that the obligation to be a resource but not an interference is just as preoccupying as the attention one gives to one's own children."

John 9:4

"We must work the works of him who sent me while it is day; night is coming when no one can work."

Erroneous Opinion

I read this somewhere: "The advantage of having lived a long time is much less important than it seems at first."

When I filed this, I suppose I was thinking about the way older people sometimes like to pontificate, as if having been wrong about something for a very long time somehow makes them right after all.

But looking at this item again, I conclude that living a long time is considerably more advantageous than not living a long time.

Psalm 91:16

With long life I will satisfy them, and show them my salvation.

"Progress"

Research at Boston College takes note of how Americans are bombarded after our fiftieth birthdays by messages telling us we are old, old, old.

The messages range from flyers in the mail that promote retirement villages to the way clerks in stores respond. Or to the way younger people's eyes glaze over when we start to offer an opinion or tell a story.

There are still cultures in other parts of the world where older people are honored and their advice is sought. But their young people have begun watching television and are becoming "Westernized." They call it "progress."

---

2 Timothy 5:17

> *Let the elders who rule well be considered worthy of double honor.*

What to Say

An old joke about advertising jingles: "If you can't think of anything to say, sing it." This inspired the following, to be sung to a tune of your choice:

Can't think what to say

To friends whose skies turn gray?

Write, "Sorry," anyway.

Love's easy to convey.

Job 6:14

"Those who withhold kindness from a friend forsake the fear of the Almighty."

Cooking

Grandpa has always liked cooking on camping trips, although at home he sees no reason to interfere in the routinely excellent conduct of culinary affairs.

He finds himself in harmony with the spirit of such movies as *Babette's Feast, Like Water for Chocolate,* and *The Big Night.* The plots vary, but the themes are the same: food is for sharing and the most important ingredient is love —never mind a sprinkling of wind-blown sand and a boiled ant or two.

Psalm 78:25

Mortals ate of the bread of angels; (the
Lord) sent them food in abundance.

High Water

When the local river spilled over its banks, we explored the flood plain in a canoe. We crossed roads where traffic no longer ran. The picnic tables in the park formed an archipelago for grandchildren to discover, like Columbus or Captain Cook.

When the kids landed on some of the "islands," they saw natives with six or even eight legs hiding in the cracks.

Mark 1:8

"I have baptized you with water; but he will baptize you with the Holy Spirit."

Amen

Some grandparents are old enough to have agitated for modernization of the rites in one denomination or another. The results sometimes recall the adage, "Be careful what you pray for. You might get it."

Poet Kathleen Norris, author of prize-winning *Dakota* and *Cloister Walk*, says it is time for less "word bombardment" and more poetic language in church.

"It's depressing, though not particularly surprising, that contemporary scholars and theologians should not be able to tell the difference between good poetry and bad, or know that there are fairly objective ways to make the distinction."

Psalm 49:4

I will incline my ear to a proverb; I will solve my riddle to the music of the harp.

Scenario for 21st Century: I

Few grandfathers will play much of a role in the twenty-first century. The new century will be primarily the era of our grandchildren.

What kind of a world will they live in? Scholars have outlined a variety of scenarios. One possibility is a world that's like a dysfunctional family.

In this forcast, technological progress, globalization and continued consumerism make some people healthier and wealthier, while misery increases for the majority. This leads to uprisings in many places and a massive shift of populations as millions flee conflicts or seek entry into more prosperous regions.

Leviticus 19:13

You shall not defraud your neighbor; you shall not steal; and you shall not keep for yourself the wages of a laborer until morning.

Scenario for 21st Century: II

Forces already active around the planet could make our grandchildren's future a new Dark Age. In this scenario, many nations splinter into smaller states defined by ethnicity or religion. The new states emphasize group think and squash individual rights.

Defensive tariffs return, crippling international trade. The collapse of global communications hampers scientific research and slows the diffusion of new technology that could help with ecological and other worldwide problems.

Mark 3:24

If a kingdom is divided against itself, that kingdom cannot stand.

Scenario for 21st Century: III

As our grandchildren live out their lives in the next century, likely disasters such as global climate change, air and water pollution and the spread of new, drug-resistant diseases will give them pause.

Just as people in the past came to reject slavery, the people of the twenty-first century could reject the kind of economic development that despoils the planet. They may come to feel that somewhat less consumerism is worthwhile.

This heightened sensitivity to the problems facing all people on the planet could lead to new interest in the teachings of the great religions. Ironically, one technological advance—the connection of nearly everyone everywhere via telecommunications—may facilitate the spread of these ancient teachings.

Mark 3:35

"Whoever does the will of God is my brother and sister and mother."

Scenario for 21st Century: IV

Spiritual and material growth aren't mutually exclusive. If globalization in the twenty-first century extends a degree of prosperity to most places, our grandchildren could see a decline in nationalism as a destructive emotional force. Differences of race, class, caste and religion also could lose their power to provoke hatred.

As people come to know each other directly in cyberspace, the residents of adjacent nations would be no more likely to fire rockets at each other than citizens of Illinois and Wisconsin. They might even pray together.

Psalm 128:1-2

Happy is everyone who fears the Lord, who walks in his ways. You shall eat the fruit of the labor of your hands; you shall be happy, and it shall go well with you.

Thanks for the Memory

Years ago, comedian Bob Hope went home for a visit with relatives in England. He threw a party for about 40 of them at a pub. When Hope got up to tell some jokes, he noticed that his grandfather, a retired stone mason, wasn't laughing.

"You're doing it wrong," the old man said. "You don't know these people. You've been a tourist. Let me do the introductions."

Hope recalled, "He was ninety-six then and, believe me, he was a ball of fire—George Jessel with an English accent."

Psalm 73:24

You guide me with your counsel, and afterward you will receive me with honor.

Slow Boat to China

Harbor scene: we pass a gray-haired man steering a high-quality inflatable boat with a big engine at dead slow speed. A small girl pokes her head and arms out of her life jacket like a turtle while she holds a long string that tows a small toy boat.

The toy is obviously homemade. It's just a small plank, with a sharp bow and a couple of blocks on top for deck houses. Since it floats upright, there must be some sort of keel weight underwater.

I grin and wave. This grandpa, obviously a soft touch for his granddaughter, was providing an expensive tugboat.

---

1 Chronicles 16:32

Let the sea roar, and all that fills it; let the field exult, and everything in it.

Thanks a Lot, Gramps

We are preparing jail cells for at least nine percent of our grandsons.

That's based on a study by the U.S. Department of Justice, projecting recent federal and state incarceration rates to American children born today.

The statistics are understated, because the study didn't include juvenile detention centers or county jails, which process thirty times as many prisoners as federal and state prisons.

We grandfathers become jailers by yielding to hysteria about crime and voting for politicians who criminalize more and more kinds of conduct and legislate longer and longer sentences.

Matthew 25:39-40

"And when was it that we saw you sick or in prison and visited you?" And the king will answer them, "Truly I tell you, just as you did it to one of the least of these who are members of my family, you did it to me."

Sailing Lesson

On an overcast day, the sky seemed dark for a small sailboat to be out. Because the sun wasn't shining, a grandson elected to stay home. But the weather bureau foresaw no violent squalls, and I put to sea anyway.

Like many things in life, the day turned out much better than expected, with a delightful steady breeze.

Psalm 46:2

> *Therefore we will not fear, though the earth should change, though the mountains shake in the heart of the sea.*

What If

A good game to play with grandchildren, once they're old enough to have learned something in school, is Alternative History.

Ask them what they think life would be like now:

• If property had traditionally passed from mother to daughter in western civilization instead of from father to son.

• If the Cherokee tribe, with their written language and organized government, had been allowed to remain in the Southeast and preserve Native American land rights in their own state.

• If Americans had joined the British in suppressing the slave trade after 1807.

Matthew 6:24

"No one can serve two masters; for a slave will either hate the one and love the other, or be devoted to the one and despise the other. You cannot serve God and wealth."

Street Smart

When grandchildren reach a certain age, they need to hear words of wisdom from their grandfather.

I tell them when trouble starts at a party or draws a crowd on the street to leave and go home before the cops come.

Police called to the scene of a disturbance can't know who has been doing what. If you're not there, you can't be among the disturbers.

Psalm 27:12

Do not give me up to the will of my adversaries, for false witnesses have risen against me, and they are breathing out violence.

Survivors

After enjoying a swashbuckling historical movie with my grandchildren, I reflect that most people alive today are descended from people who tried to avoid such danger and excitement.

Our ancestors were probably the ones who hid out in the woods when barbarians ran amok or who sneaked out a rear gate in the dark when a city was besieged.

Matthew 26:52

Then Jesus said to him, "Put your sword back into its place; for all who take the sword will perish by the sword."

Reincarnation?

Looking at family photos, I see grandchildren who look like their ancestors. Sometimes there's a likeness close enough almost to suggest reincarnation. Sometimes just a fleeting expression recalls the seriousness of the Depression or the merriment of the Jazz Age.

We know something of how our ancestors' lives turned out. Some were worthy of emulation by all their descendants.

Others had their weaknesses. Maybe the grandchildren who look most like them will be the ones to do better.

Not everything is genetic.

Colossians 3:17

And whatever you do, in word or deed, do everything in the name of the Lord Jesus, giving thanks to God the Father through him.

Boys' Toys

Having sons has traditionally given fathers an excuse to play with electric trains and other traditional boys' toys.

Having grandsons today lets grandfathers play with toys that, half a century ago, hadn't been invented yet.

Here comes the remote-controlled toy fire truck containing a computer chip that makes realistic noises. Stand back. It's so realistic it even squirts water.

Gotcha.

Job 8:21

He will yet fill your mouth with laughter, and your lips with shouts of joy.

Manners

Sir John of the Red Face looked out an arrow slit in the castle tower and saw the his sons brawling again. "It's time they were sent off to another castle to learn manners," he said to his wife. She agreed. So he promptly arranged a swap of teen-age boys with his neighbor, three for three.

That's how they coped with adolescence in olden days. After a few years as pages in some-one else's household, the young men would return home as what passed for gentlemen—at a time when people cut their meat with their daggers and threw what they didn't want to the dogs under the table.

Now that castles are out of date, it's still possible for grandparents to take young people away from home—at least for short periods, during which hints on manners can be gently dropped.

Leviticus 19:32

You shall rise before the aged, and defer to the old; and you shall fear your God: I am the LORD.

Kidistan

In the country of Kidistan, children are in charge. Schools close for especially nice days as well as blizzards and ice storms. Government inspectors prevent restaurants from ever serving any dish that could be considered yucky.

There's a play lot in every block, to which grandfathers are required to report weekly for the purpose of pushing grandchildren in swings.

Numbers 14:8

If the Lord is pleased with us, he will bring us into this land and give it to us, a land that flows with milk and honey.

Melting Pot

A young man brings a girl to meet his grandfather from the old country. The young man explains, haltingly in the language Grandpa understands, that he wishes to introduce his fiancée.

She sees an old man in an easy chair with a glass of wine at his elbow. He's wearing an ill-fitting suit jacket bought eons ago in one of Europe's less prosperous countries.

There's a chance here for missteps all round. The bride-to-be could snub an odd-looking immigrant. The grandfather could disapprove of the intrusion of a different ethnic group into the clan.

Instead, the grandfather stands, bows and lifts his glass in a toast—not just to the engagement but also to the future great-grandchildren who will come to play around his knees.

Psalm 33:13

The LORD looks down from heaven; he sees all humankind.

Messages to the Future

I write down significant thoughts and quotations in my journal. Sometimes when I come back to them later I'm not sure why I thought them so interesting.

Somewhere I read, "Children are living messages we send to a time we'll never see."

That's true enough, but what is the message? That Grandpa was never grouchy? Never said mean things about anyone? Never even cursed other drivers?

Well, almost never.

James 4:14-15

Yet you do not even know what tomorrow will bring. What is your life? For you are a mist that appears for a little while and then vanishes. Instead you ought to say, "If the Lord wishes, we will live and do this or that."

Champion

Barclay Howard, a Scottish golfer, qualified for the U.S. Amateur Open. Then he noticed that he had accidentally broken the rules by using two different kinds of golf balls.

No one else knew, but he pointed out the error to officials, knowing he would lose his chance to compete in the tournament.

Philippians 4:8

Finally, beloved, whatever is true, whatever is honorable, whatever is just, whatever is pure, whatever is pleasing, whatever is commendable, if there is any excellence and if there is anything worthy of praise, think about these things.

Heart Medicine

A new study says that men who think of themselves as failures or feel hopeless for whatever reason are more likely than others to develop atherosclerosis. (That's a narrowing of the arteries that leads to heart attacks and strokes.)

Sometimes, when grandchildren grow noisy and overactive, a grandfather might be tempted to say, "You kids are going to give me a heart attack!"

In truth, it's the other way round. Healthy grandchildren, representing hope for the future, may actually help prevent such a catastrophe.

Psalm 31:24

Be strong, and let your heart take courage, all you who wait for the LORD.

Hot Bibles

Religious book sales in the U.S. are booming, accounting for one-quarter of all adult titles.

But Christian bookstore managers report they have just as big a problem with shoplifting as anyone else.

In fact, more Bibles are stolen than any other book.

What do thieves do with the Bibles, read them or sell them? "Psst, wanna buy a hot Bible?"

Ephesians 4:28

Thieves must give up stealing; rather let them labor and work honestly with their own hands, so as to have something to share with the needy.

International Relations

When the newspapers reported something of a baby boom in Moscow, commentators said that was a sign young couples were feeling more hopeful about the future of Russia.

I thought of all the new Russian grandfathers celebrating the arrival of a new Ivan or Natasha.

Regardless of the ebb and flow of political tensions between Moscow and Washington, I'd be happy to link arms and sip a glass of vodka with them.

As they say in Russia on such occasions, *"Pazdravlyáyu!"*

---

1 Samuel 20:42

> *"Go in peace, since both of us have sworn in the name of the LORD, saying 'The LORD shall be between me and you, and between my descendents and your descendents, forever.'"*

Forgiving

Grandfathers should be doubly tolerant of the transgressions of grandchildren.

First, a grandpa should be able to remember when he himself in first grade pushed crayons against the radiator to see how sparkly the colors became when the wax melted and ran down the metal, blue, red, yellow, orange, purple.

Second, he can remember when his own child, who has since become an energetic and successful adult, could never be cajoled, threatened or forced into finishing homework. Thumbscrews might have worked, but they were no longer readily available.

Matthew 6:14

"For if you forgive others their trespasses, your heavenly Father will also forgive you."

Retirement

Sooner or later, grandfathers have to think about retiring.

But it's better to retire *to* something than *from* something.

Men who can retire to spend more time with grandchildren are better off than men who have no grandchildren, or none within reach.

Numbers 8:25

From the age of fifty years they shall retire from the duty of the service and serve no more

Shepherds

In moments of self-doubt, every grandfather wonders whether he was a good enough father to his own children.

The short answer is: everyone regrets some failures or shortcomings.

But when a grandfather sees a son or daughter treating a grandchild in a wise and loving way, Grandpa is entitled to think, "Well, I must have done some things right."

Psalm 78:52

*Then he led out his people like sheep,
and guided them in the wilderness like
a flock.*

Undepressed

Just before the Depression hit, Great-Grandpa sold the farm. Somehow, he was wise enough or lucky enough to put the money in a bank that didn't collapse.

So he was able to be generous. Rather than see his long-time neighbors lose their farms and homes, he paid their property taxes until times improved.

It's not known whether he eventually got all his money back. But either way, his heirs enjoy a splendid heritage.

Matthew 5:7

"Blessed are the merciful, for they will receive mercy."

Like Grandfather, Like Grandson?

The young man is charming. Everybody likes him and will buy whatever he's selling this month. That varies because he changes jobs frequently. People who knew his grandfather say the old man was the same, always launching big plans that never worked out either.

Because of exciting progress in the study of genetics, the current tendency is to blame everything on genes. But Stephen Jay Gould, a noted biologist, says an either/or approach to nature vs. nurture "verges on the nonsensical."

There's still time for any young man to focus on a dream and make it happen.

Genesis 16:8

"Where have you come from and where are you going?"

Exuberance

I wouldn't be surprised if there were some wise grandfathers involved in the decision of Freeport, Maine, to build skateboard ramps on part of the high school parking lot.

Kids on skateboards have become a nuisance, zooming down crowded sidewalks and through shopping malls. They menace fragile older people and small children.

The usual response is to pass restrictive ordinances, assess fines and encourage police to harass kids more than they already do. But the natural exuberance of youth has to come out somehow.

It's interesting that in Freeport, with so many kids busy on the skateboard ramps, police have noted a drop in crime.

Psalm 119:39
Turn away the disgrace that I dread,
for your ordinances are good.

By the Book

Gifts of books to grandchildren can be lessons in living.

Almost any well-written story about little furry animals teaches compassion.

Mark Twain's *The Adventures of Huckleberry Finn,* criticized by some ever since it was first published, is about faithfulness. The Narnia books by C.S. Lewis teach morals without moralizing. E.B. White's *Charlotte's Web* helps children come to grips with death.

Psalm 25:4

> *Make me to know your ways, O Lord;*
> *teach me your paths.*

Treadmill

"I've told those kids not to do that a thousand times," someone says.

One definition of insanity: doing same thing over and over and expecting a different result.

Proverbs 17:16
Why should fools have a price in hand to buy wisdom, when they have no mind to learn?

A Journey

My grandfather once sent me money to travel to Pittsburgh from Chicago. He must have wanted to see me.

His reward was that I drove his car all over and used up lots of gas at a time when gas was hard to get.

As I grew older, I realized that I must have been rather a nuisance.

As I grew even older, I understood why he didn't seem to think so.

He was my grandfather.

Psalm 25:18

*Consider my affliction and my trouble,
and forgive all my sins.*

Survival Skills

The "civilized" Swedes recently did penance for a time when they sterilized people to eliminate "inferior breeds."

Grandpas get to philosophize. Who's to say who's inferior?

Do we want to breed more people with the skills that allow fugurative big fish to eat little fish?

Or, in a future that seems to strain the resources of the planet, perhaps people more inclined to cooperate and share with other small fish will be the most desirable survivors.

---

2 Corinthians 9:7

Each of you must give as you have made up your mind, not reluctantly or under compulsion, for God loves a cheerful giver.

An Argument for Humility

At least one prominent biologist joins many grandparents in fearing that scientists may come up with something that interferes with human evolutionary development and pretty much wipes us out.

That would turn the planet over not to our descendants, but to beetles, of which there are at least two hundred thousand different species.

Daniel 5:28

Your kingdom is divided and given to the Medes and Persians.

Beyond Words

A small girl arrives at a big family picnic, the kind with a rented tent and hordes of out-of-town relatives she's never seen before. She's frightened.

Then she sees Grandpa, down on one knee with his arms extended to gather her up with a hug. She runs to him, smiling.

A California social scientist, quoted by United Press International, says a hug is a form of communication that says things you don't have words for.

Mark 10:16

And (Jesus) took them up in his arms, laid his hands on them, and blessed them.

Honorary Grandpas

Some leading theoreticians in the field of biology are saying that recent dramatic discoveries in genetic research obscure the fact that the whole is still greater than the sum of the parts.

"Knowing the sequence of individual genes doesn't tell you anything about the complexities of what life is," says Dr. Brian Goodwin, a British scientist.

In this day of divorces, remarriages and other family rearrangements, "Grandpa" is not always really the grandfather, but a grandchild is always a grandchild.

Psalm 36:9

For with you is the fountain of life; in your light we see light.

Genealogy Lesson

People who poke around in their family history sooner or later find out something they might rather not know.

One writer, proud of her Irish ancestry, always resented the brutal suppression of Irish freedom by the English under Oliver Cromwell. Then her research revealed that she was descended from one of Cromwell's soldiers, who had been given nine acres of land in Ireland for his services.

Despite such potential embarrassments, passing on the family history to grandchildren is an important duty of grandparents.

---

2 Samuel 7:12

When your days are fulfilled and you lie down with your ancestors, I will raise up your offspring after you, who shall come forth from your body, and I will establish his kingdom.

Attention

A small girl stood in front of a group of adults. She read aloud a list of riddles for them to guess the answers. Mostly, they guessed wrong. She was delighted to set them straight, basking in the focus of attention from parents, aunts and uncles, and grandpa.

An excellent way for a girl to celebrate her birthday!

---

1 Corinthians 5:8

Therefore, let us celebrate the festival, not with the old yeast, the yeast of malice and evil, but with the unleavened bread of sincerity and truth.

Games

If I think grandchildren are still young enough to cry if they lose, I let them win. As they grow older, I play my best. It's no fun for anyone to beat someone who isn't trying.

Throughout life, there are times to try to keep people from being unhappy and times to compete so that the winner can know the thrill of accomplishment.

Someday, if one of my granddaughters becomes a professional basketball player, maybe she'll remember this: although victory is the reward of effort, winning *isn't* everything.

Ecclesiastes 9:11

Again I saw that under the sun the race is not to the swift, nor the battle to the strong, nor the wise, nor bread to the wise, nor riches to the intelligent, nor favor to the skillful; but time and chance happen to them all.

No Neckties, Please

The first Sunday after Labor Day is National Grandparents Day.

So far, it doesn't get nearly as much attention as Mothers Day or Fathers Day. The reason is that merchants haven't moved in on it...yet.

But it is proper that a day be set aside to take notice of grandparents. Ex-President Jimmy Carter has said: "Our senior generation also provides our society a link to our national heritage and traditions."

Romans 12:10

Love one another with mutual affection; outdo one another in showing honor.

A Touch of Power

Writing in a popular magazine, a California social scientist says a person needs "four hugs a day for survival, eight for maintenance and twelve for growth."

Hugs transfer the kind of psychic energy that's good for the spirit. People know instinctively that hugging small children helps them thrive.

When you're a grandfather, hugging provides a bonus: grandchildren hug you back.

Luke 6:19

And all in the crowd were trying to touch him, for power came out from him and healed all of them.

Sympathy

(Scene: a store. Cast: a five-year-old girl, her grandfather and another customer, who is severely handicapped.)

GIRL (addressing woman): What happened to you?

GRANDPA (aside): Good grief! How do I smooth this over without embarrassment?

WOMAN: It's a long story.

GIRL: Well, tell me half of it.

---

1 Timothy 4:12

Let no one despise your youth, but set the believers an example in speech and conduct, in love, in faith, in purity.

Possibilities

In college I might have prepared to become a natural history museum curator, but I never saw a course in the catalog anything like "Jungle Exploring 101." It never occurred to me to ask a faculty member for advice.

Grandfathers, with long experience of life, can help grandchildren see alternatives both in daily life and in career choices that they might not think of. And coming from Grandpa, instead of parents, such advice may be taken, or at least considered, without controversy.

Psalm 16:7

I bless the LORD who gives me counsel;
in the night also my heart instructs me.

Any Other Name

The birth of a child is usually accompanied by intensive discussion of possible names. After all that, it soon turns out that Francesca wants to be called "Frikki" or possibly "Jojo."

Grandpa, however, can usually get away with using the official given name. And when the grandchild grows up, begins thinking about a career and wanting to go back to being Francesca, Grandpa is credited with foresight.

Numbers 27:1

> *Then the daughters of Zelophehad came forward. Zelophehad was son of Hepher son of Gilead son of Machir son of Manasseh son of Joseph, a member of the Manassite clans. The names of his daughters were: Mahlah, Noah, Hoglah, Milcah, and Tirzah.*

Grandpets

Watching a bull elk graze, I recall that people have been fascinated by animals ever since our ancestors started painting them on cave walls. It's no wonder children everywhere crave pets.

A pet is an animal that can love them uncritically, play with them on demand and give them a moment of feeling in control at an age when everyone else is telling them what to do.

Come to think of it, a grandpa can be a lot like a pet.

Genesis 7:8-9

Of clean animals, and of animals that are not clean, and of birds, and of everything that creeps on the ground, two and two, male and female, went into the ark with Noah, as God had commanded Noah.

Art Lesson

Leo Lionni, the famous children's book artist, claimed in a newspaper interview that he has always had trouble relating to individual children. But in the next breath he spoke of the "shocking discovery" that a two-year-old can be a person.

"I always thought of two-year-olds as babies," he said. But his two-year-old grandson "has the kind of style the others don't have. He chooses the clothes for (a sibling)."

By recognizing that tiny children are indeed distinct persons, Lionni set an example for other grandfathers.

Proverbs 27:17

Iron sharpens iron, and one person sharpens the wits of another.

Another Art Lesson

Leo Lionni was working in advertising when he had to amuse his young grandchildren on a slow commuter train ride to Greenwich, Connecticut. To keep them quiet, he made up a story and tore out pieces from a magazine to illustrate it.

That story became the first of his many distinguished books for children.

Many artists and writers have started like this, amusing one or two children close to them, then reaching out to entertain thousands of others.

Grandchildren teach grandpas as well as learn from them.

Proverbs 1:5

Let the wise also hear and gain in learning.

Aptitude Test for Grandpas

Questions for expectant grandfathers:

Out for a walk, you come to a block where most of the houses have neatly trimmed lawns surrounded by flowers. One house stands out because the front yard is littered with balls, toy trucks and a mysterious construction of cardboard boxes. A tricycle on its side sprawls across the sidewalk.

If you smile at the evidence of happy children recently playing, you pass the Test.

If you grumble to yourself that these people ought to take better care of their front yard, you need to go to a boot camp for grandpas.

Luke 18:16

> *"Let the little children come to me, and do not stop them; for it is to such as these that the kingdom of God belongs."*

The Critic

A grandchild sits absorbed with a sheet of paper and a box of crayons. After a time, she passes a drawing across the table and says, "This is for you, Grandpa."

A large round circle has jug-handle ears and dots for eyes to identify it as a head. There is a fringe of hair above the ears, but none on top.

"It looks just like me," he says proudly.

Grandpa knows better than to ask, "What is it?"

Colossians 1:15

*He is the image of the invisible God,
the firstborn of all creation.*

Old Story

When grandparents get together, they often discuss what seems like a decline in manners among the younger generation. They may want to know that, as long ago as 1530, Erasmus of Rotterdam, the great scholar and philosopher, took time to write a book of etiquette for children that was in print for two centuries.

In a cruder age, his admonitions included such items as this one: "Do not move back and forth in your chair. Whoever does that gives the impression of constantly breaking or trying to break wind."

Philippians 4:9

Keep on doing the things that you have learned and received and heard and seen in me, and the God of peace will be with you.

Wrong Decision

Marine weather forecast for children: "Wind from the southwest five to ten knots. Fifty percent chance of hot, boring afternoon in barely moving sailboat while Grandpa tries to convince you that you're having a good time."

Hearing this, I decide not to invite one or two grandchildren to go out with me in the small sailboat I built in the garage.

But the wind turns out to be steady from the southeast, which means an afternoon of steady, fast sailing. I deeply repent I didn't urge the grandkids to come.

Sirach 44:16

Enoch pleased the Lord and was taken up, an example of repentance to all generations.

Grandpa as Guru

New research shows teens listen to parents more than they seem to.

Despite the outward rebelliousness, they are still the same kids inside, still absorbing their parents' values.

Although the researchers didn't look into it, grandpas too probably have more influence than they think.

Luke 21:38

And all the people would get up early in the morning to listen to him in the temple.

Cakes at Dawn

It's true that in our times most children get too much Stuff for their birthdays. We live in an age generally characterized by too much of everything (including, paradoxically, poverty.)

But we don't begin to give children the kind of birthday blast they enjoyed in thirteenth century Germany. Then the *Kinderfeste* began at dawn when the birthday child was wakened by a cake with lighted candles. As the candles burned down during the day, they were replaced and kept lit until the cake was eaten after dinner.

The child also received gifts and was allowed to choose the dinner menu.

John 16:21

When a woman is in labor, she has pain, because her hour has come. But when her child is born, she no longer remembers the anguish because of the joy of having brought a human being into the world.

Legacy

Grandfathers can never tell how far their influence will reach. One day in 1913, Arthur Wynne was ordered to think of a new game for the Sunday edition of the *New York World*.

He remembered an old word-square game his grandfather had taught him, in which the words read the same horizontally and vertically. Wynne thought of varying it by providing blank squares and a list of clues.

In this way, Wynne's grandfather helped Wynne invent crossword puzzles. They remain popular to this day almost everywhere (except in countries like China that don't have ABCs).

Proverbs 3:1

My child, do not forget my teaching, but let your heart keep my commandments.

The Human Condition

Such a beautiful child. Backlighting makes a halo of her tawny hair as she stares, utterly absorbed by a flower.

No wonder they call little children angels, thinks her grandfather. She could be one of the cherubs from a Renaissance fresco.

Then he notices that she needs her pants changed.

Matthew 18:4

Whoever becomes humble like this child is the greatest in the kingdom of heaven.

Somebody's Grandchildren

On Rikers Island, where New York operates the world's largest prison, the city spends seventy thousand dollars a year to lock up each juvenile. That's nearly ten times the budget for each child in the city's public school system.

Some of these prisoners no doubt need to be locked up to protect society. But doesn't it seem that if some qualified grandfather took charge of, say, three of these kids and was given over two hundred thousand a year to spend, something better could be done?

Wouldn't that much money buy these kids a fair amount of drug and alcohol treatment, education and job training?

Psalm 142:7

> *Bring me out of prison, so that I may give thanks to your name. The righteous will surround me, for you will deal bountifully with me.*

Happy Ending

In the original version of "Little Red Riding Hood," as written down in 1697 by Charles Perrault, both Granny and Red Riding Hood were eaten by the wolf, and that was that.

Revisions by other story-tellers soon began to include different endings in which Red Riding Hood escapes. But it took 120 years to spare Granny. In the Grimm Brothers version, a passing hunter cuts open the wolf in time to save both Red Riding Hood and Granny.

The grandfathers' lobby finally made its influence felt.

John 10:11-12

> *"I am the good shepherd. The good shepherd lays down his life for the sheep. The hired hand, who is not the shepherd and does not own the sheep, sees the wolf coming and leaves the sheep and runs away."*

Ethical Dilemma

Small boy extorts a toy from his younger sister. She pinches him. Daddy observes the pinch but not the theft, so he scolds her.

Grandpa, who has seen it all, wonders which course to take. Should he risk acquiring a reputation as a snitch? Or should he take a stand for justice?

Nobody promised grandfathering would be simple.

John 2:25

(Jesus) needed no one to testify about anyone; for he himself knew what was in everyone.

So Long to Summer

Why do people make a fuss about the first day of Autumn? When the Sun crosses the Equator (or, more accurately, the Equator crosses the Sun), there's nothing to see. The weather today will be much like yesterday.

What captures attention is the symbolism of the days growing shorter. Not just the days of the year but also the days of our lives.

It is our grandchildren who will greet the Spring long into the twenty-first century.

Psalm 90:10

*The days of our life are seventy years,
or perhaps eighty, if we are strong;
even then their span is only toil and
trouble; they are soon gone, and we fly
away.*

Teasing Grandpa

She snatched off Grandpa's hat and ran with it, giggling. He chased her and caught her, recapturing his hat and putting it back on his bald head.

She was surprised that the old man could still catch her, the fastest girl runner in her class.

So was he.

He inadvertently grabbed her hair in the process instead of the scruff of her jacket.

But she didn't mind. She enjoyed the attention.

So did he.

Psalm 18:33

> *He made my feet like the feet of a deer,*
> *and set me secure on the heights.*

Skywriting

Walking home from eighth grade, I was aston-
ished to see the sky raining pants, sweaters,
shirts. I recognized them as my own, all of which
I had left on the floor of my room as usual.

When I looked up, I saw my mother taking
aim at me from my window with a football jersey.
Good thing she didn't notice the cleated shoes
under the bed!

I no longer recall whether it was that experience or service in the Navy that changed me,
but to this day I am scrupulous about hanging up
my clothes. I mention this, out of a grandfather's
gift of long memory, when my grandchildren are
criticized for their messy rooms.

Reform is possible.

Ephesians 4:22, 24

*You were taught to put away your
former way of life...and to clothe
yourselves with the new self, created
according to the likeness of God in true
righteousness and holiness.*

Courage

With weeping and wailing, the little granddaughter resists being left at pre-school. She says, precociously, "It's a long day for a four-year-old."

Finally, with reassuring cuddling from Mommy and Daddy, she settles down.

The teacher, after all, is sweetly competent. And in the corner a statue of Joan of Arc looks on approvingly.

---

2 Timothy 1:7

For God did not give us a spirit of cowardice, but rather a spirit of power and of love and of self-discipline.

Due Process

By now, I assume somebody's lawyer-grandpa has done something about a West Coast community that applies what they call "tough love" to kids as young as twelve years old in the county jail.

Awaiting trial, these kids are shackled to stainless steel benches, strip searched, locked up two to a cell with nothing to read but "religious texts" and forced to lie face down to "kiss the linoleum" as long as guards feel like it.

Some of these children will be found not guilty. But all of the officials responsible for this outrage are criminals of a sort, having disregarded the U. S. Constitution, which frowns on punishment without due process.

Why has it become so hard to love kids and so easy to get tough with them?

Psalm 109:3

They beset me with words of hate, and attack me without cause.

"Tell Me a Story"

Before books were invented, grandpas were the source of inspirational tales.

Then for centuries, children who could read had to make do with adult books. *Aesop's Fables* from ancient Greece was one of the few with natural appeal to the young.

In 1563 came an illustrated book by John Foxe about Christian martyrs. Grandfathers read it to grandchildren to help them learn to read. Focusing on various stonings, floggings, beheadings and boilings in oil, it offered almost as many lurid details as television.

Fortunately children still say, "Tell me (or read me) a story, Grandpa."

Nehemiah 8:8

So they read from the book, from the law of God, with interpretation. They gave the sense, so that the people understood the reading.

Trio Con Brio

The three stages of life:

1. Playing music so loud it annoys parents.

2. Yelling at children to turn down the volume (or possibly trying to communicate with signs because they can't possibly hear).

3. Witnessing the above and recalling that the persons now doing the yelling were not so long ago the recipients of critical comments themselves regarding excessive *fortissimo*.

Leviticus 19:18

You shall not take vengeance or bear a grudge against any of your people, but you shall love your neighbor as yourself: I am the LORD.

Praise God

Watching the faces of the children's choir in church, I wonder how they visualize the God whose praises they sing. Do some still think of God as the old man with a beard on the ceiling of the Sistine Chapel?

Or do they grasp the idea of a perfect love by analogy to the well-intentioned but imperfect love they receive from their grandpas?

Since I wasn't allowed to keep the beard I started to grow on the summer's canoe trip, I don't look much like God.

But I can try to offer enough love to make an impact.

Psalm 42:2

My soul thirsts for God, for the living God. When shall I come and behold the face of God?

Careers

I remember myself as a student walking through the outskirts of town out into the desert. In the early dark, I pass houses where families can be seen through the lighted windows gathered for dinner.

Beyond the last house, on a road lit dimly by stars, I ponder what I will be doing after this last year of school and where I will be living. What's at the end of this road?

Now I sit in my own dining room, and such musings are for my grandchildren.

Jeremiah 31:17

There is hope for your future, says the LORD: your children shall come back to their own country.

His Majesty Grandpa

Some of the most democratic, civilized and progressive nations of northwestern Europe retain their monarchies. To Americans, who like to think no one is better than anyone else, the idea of royalty seems a strange anachronism.

But the people of those nations like their monarchies because the king/queen is a sort of national grandfather/grandmother. He or she embodies their national history and traditions and confers legitimacy upon changing governments.

Psalm 61:6

Prolong the life of the king; may his years endure to all generations!

Winds

On the last sailing day of the season, the winds are light and variable. We glide a little, then stop, the boom swinging with the motion of the waves. The grandchildren are bored and restless. We motor in early.

Maybe they're learning that sailing is like life. There's a prevailing wind that's often predictable. But there are also other winds that blow from unexpected directions, sometimes with overwhelming force.

And boredom too is part of life,

Psalm 78:39

He remembered that they were but flesh, a wind that passes and does not come again.

The "Morfar"

In his acclaimed memoir of his youth, *Stop Time,* Frank Conroy, who became a successful novelist and teacher of other writers, tells of meeting his Danish grandfather for the first time. Conroy spoke no Danish, the grandfather no English. But the grandfather "nevertheless managed to convey his interest in me." That surprised Conroy as a teenager.

Any grandfather understands that Conroy's *morfar* (Danish for mother's father), described as a small, gentle man, was passionately interested in his young grandson from America and frustrated that all he could do to communicate was talk louder in Danish, pat him on the back and try to get him to eat more food.

Judges 12:14
He had forty sons and thirty grandsons.

Missing Guest

We expected a guest for dinner. The short notice was no problem. We had food on hand we knew she liked. We looked forward to an interesting conversation.

Then it turned out the guest couldn't come after all. Her mother explained that the guest was cranky, not having napped properly in pre-school.

I was surprised at how much I was disappointed.

Hebrews 13:2

Do not neglect to show hospitality to strangers, for by doing that some have entertained angels without knowing it.

Changes

When I first moved to the community where I live now, the main street petered out into a narrow two-lane road just north of town. The road dipped to cross a small creek over a wooden bridge just wide enough for one car—or farm tractor.

Now the little creek flows through concrete tubes under subdivisions, shopping malls and parking lots. The old country road has become a four-lane roadway. It all happened so little at a time that I scarcely noticed.

I try to tell my grandchildren about such observations to give them a notion of the many changes they can expect in their lives.

Romans 15:4

For whatever was written in former days was written for our instruction, so that by steadfastness and by the encouragement of the scriptures we might have hope.

Opera in One Act

(An automobile glides onto the stage like the swan boat in Wagner's *Lohengrin*. A young man follows it and walks to the driver's door.)

TENOR

> My license did arrive, tra-la.
>
> Now watch me drive, tra-la, tra-la.

CHORUS OF GRANDFATHERS

> Stay alive, stay alive.
>
> Whatever dumb thing you think to do
>
> It's likely we once did it too.
>
> That's why we chant again to you:
>
> Stay alive, stay alive.

Psalm 1:6

> *For the LORD watches over the way of the righteous, but the way of the wicked will perish.*

Legacy

After retiring from business, the old man spent twenty years as an enthusiastic volunteer for community organizations. At his funeral service, his eldest grandson spoke lovingly of the grandfather who always found time to listen to him, who always made him feel that he was an important and special person, even as a small child and only one of a dozen grandchildren.

What he learned from his grandfather, the young man said, was that "a well-lived life is an inspiration."

Psalm 101:2

I will study the way that is blameless. When shall I attain it? I will walk with integrity of heart within my house.

Goals

Not many American grandfathers grew up playing soccer. We played football, softball and basketball. In the city, vacant lots were too small for real baseball. A good hitter could too easily bang a hardball through someone's window.

Now grandchildren teach us the fine points of soccer.

That's not all they can teach us if we pay attention.

Psalm 8:2

*Out of the mouths of babes and infants
you have founded a bulwark because of
your foes, to silence the enemy and the
avenger.*

Smoothing the Way

The plain copy paper normally used in photo-copiers, computer printers and other office machines is smoother on one side than the other. Certain machines, such as inkjet printers, print better on the smooth side. That's why the package often has a label saying something like "image this side first."

With a little practice, people can feel the difference, which is useful when the paper is no longer in the package and we need to know which side should be up. In our technological society we don't rely on our physical senses enough. Actually, our senses are more acute than we realize.

We have spiritual senses too. We don't use them enough either.

---

1 Corinthians 14:1

> *Pursue love and strive for the spiritual gifts, and especially that you may prophesy.*

Fallen Leaves

In the golden days of autumn, he would drink tea with his daughter and tell his grandchildren tales of the old country. They would have to know from whom they came in order to know who they were.

The old gardener would show them how to cultivate plants that would grow and flourish like youthful dreams.

He remembers his daughter at about their ages. She couldn't decide whether she would grow up to be a ballerina or an astronaut.

Now her chair is vacant. The teapot is cold. Hearing the grandchildren's voices outdoors, he recalls there are still leaves to rake.

Isaiah 44:3

I will pour out water upon the thirsty ground, and streams upon the dry land; I will pour out my spirit upon your offspring, and my blessing upon your descendants.

Head Start

Reading to babies doesn't seem especially useful. They really can't follow the plot well enough to tell whether the cat is in the hat or the hat is in the cat (which as anyone who knows cats can testify is actually more likely).

But now comes research at Johns Hopkins University showing that babies as young as eight months can recognize and remember words.

Instead of waiting until grandchildren are old enough to play checkers, grandfathers can read to them from the beginning and start bonding at an early age.

---

2 Corinthians 1:13

For we write you nothing other than what you can read and also understand.

Evolution

Scholars are saying that grandmothers were essential to the survival of the human species in prehistoric times. Once past their child-bearing years, they were free to help forage for food for the family while not generating any more mouths to feed.

I like to think that grandfathers also were useful in their way. "Look, kid, when you need to use your backhand to hit our breakfast with your hunting axe, you should shift your grip a quarter turn, like this...."

Proverbs 4:1
Listen, children, to a father's instruction, and be attentive, that you may gain insight.

Listening

Professional counselors say a big part of their job is just listening. People with a support group of relatives and friends seem to handle stress better because they can tell their story until they tire of it themselves.

So it seemed natural for the granddaughter in preschool to call and complain to her grandpa. A naughty little boy had thrown so much sand in her eyes that she had to go to the emergency room.

The eye-flushing machine was "scary," she said. But afterwards they gave her a Popsicle.

Psalm 5:2

Listen to the sound of my cry, my King and my God, for to you I pray.

A Toast to Love

In a letter to a Chicago newspaper protesting a proposed ban on admitting children to neighborhood taverns, a woman wrote of her fond memories of going to the corner bar with her grandfather. A precinct captain and one-time minor league ball player, he enjoyed a wide acquaintance among other city workers, burly men with callused hands.

She and her brother, ages five and seven, would watch the ball game on the TV and hear Grandpa brag about them. "Such good kids, so bright!" his buddies would say.

"My brother and I still joke about the experience and the men who helped us see how much our grandpa loved us," she explained.

Psalm 4:7

*You have put gladness in my heart
more than when their grain and wine
abound.*

Fidelity

Statistics suggest that some of the grandfathers reading this book will have learned that a grandchild is homosexual. That's no reason to love him or her any less than any other grandchild.

So say many religious leaders, including the U.S. Catholic bishops. Homosexuality is a condition generally not "freely chosen," said the bishops in an official document.

The bishops issued their letter to counteract the rejection by families of a "shocking number" of homosexual young people, who then may wind up on the streets.

What a strange way to treat a child whose birth once brought so much joy.

John 13:35

> *"By this everyone will know that you are my disciples, if you have love for one another."*

Once Upon a Time

The grandtoads came to visit Grandpa and Grandma Toad. The toadlings were in a naughty mood. Having eaten too many chocolate-covered crickets in the car, they ran through the house and hopped on the furniture.

When Grandma served a dinner she thought they would enjoy, they said, "We don't like that." Their mother said, "Don't be rude," but they stuck out their tongues.

Grandpa said, "Now I will stick out *my* tongue." His tongue stretched across the room and out the window. It ran down the block to the corner, waited for the light to turn green, and crossed the street. It continued on for two more blocks until it zapped a young horsefly who insisted on eating with all six elbows on the table.

---

1 John 2:1

My little children, I am writing these things to you so that you may not sin.

Affection

The veteran principal of a girls' high school once told me that the biggest reason young girls get pregnant is that they're starved for affection. I thought of this recently when researchers said that what many delinquent boys have in common is also an absence of affection in their lives.

During the years when young people are being most difficult, it can be hard for parents to demonstrate their affection for a child who barely speaks to them and may pretend in public not even to know them.

But grandparents can inhabit a neutral country, a sort of Sweden or Switzerland in family politics, and continue to supply the uncritical affection children secretly crave.

Romans 12:10
> *Love one another with mutual affection; outdo one another in showing honor.*

Appliances

The young appliance repair man said, "I don't know whether I can get the part. I've never seen a freezer this old before." It was true. That freezer was actually older than the repair man.

And it turned out that parts were no longer available. So my wife and I bought a new freezer.

But that was some years ago. The "new" freezer, the "new" refrigerator, the "new" stove and many other "new" possessions are new only in our minds.

One of these days some young doctor will look at one of us and say, "I don't think I can get you a new part."

Psalm 71:9

Do not cast me off in the time of old age; do not forsake me when my strength is spent.

Fair-Weather Christians?

When I hear of grandpas who promise grandchildren some reward to avoid smoking or to attend Sunday school or whatever, I wonder whether that's a good idea.

I am reminded of the story of the Shakers, whose simple, hard-working lives were an attractive feature of the nineteenth century.

The Shaker communities welcomed new members into their well-built, well-provisioned settlements. But they were plagued every year by a number of people who got religion at the approach of winter, then left with the first warm days of spring.

Psalm 37:24
Though we stumble, we shall not fall headlong, for the LORD holds us by the hand.

Encores

Contrary to what we'd like to think, grandparents who have to assume full-time care of their grandchildren are twice as likely to become depressed as grandparents who don't (twenty-five percent vs. fourteen percent).

So says a new nationwide study. The stress of dealing with children full-time is combined with grief for the natural parent who has died or a sense of failure regarding the natural parent who for some reason has proven incapable of childrearing.

But, just as we would hope, these stressed caregivers speak also of the joys of watching their grandchildren grow day to day and being an intimate part of their lives.

Psalm 92:14

In old age (the righteous) still produce fruit; they are always green and full of sap.

Check

The grandfather sits smoking his pipe and playing checkers with his grandson. As the grandfather executes a triple jump, the boy says something like "gee whiz" and looks dismayed, but he's learning a lesson about life: the same rules apply to everyone, and experience is valuable.

But I don't smoke, and the game is chess, not checkers. The boy has beaten me twice in a row, and I wasn't letting him win.

So what's the lesson? Even if the price is defeat, any time spent with grandchildren is worth it.

Psalm 89:47

Remember how short my time is—for what vanity you have created all mortals!

Sticky Subject

Small children are always sticky. They exude stickiness like a rubber tree giving up its latex or a sugar maple dripping syrup.

Parents don't notice because they're used to mopping sticky hands and chins with a damp cloth in mid-sentence.

Grandpas *do* notice, because they've forgotten how it used to be. They *pretend* not to notice.

But that's only fair, because little children don't notice Grandpa's thick glasses, false teeth, blotchy skin and other signs of aging. They just come to him for hugs without comment.

Luke 6:41

"Why do you see the speck in your neighbor's eye, but do not notice the log in your own eye?"

Utility Vehicle

As men grow older, they sometimes question their usefulness. Maybe they've been forcibly retired. Or they've turned over the farm or the store to the kids.

In this country men define themselves too much in terms of their occupations.

But grandpas can remain useful just by being grandfathers. There's always a demand for someone with time to tell stories and play games.

Genesis 4:21

He was the ancestor of all those who play the lyre and the pipe.

Video Critics

Watching a well-done, entertaining rented video, the ordinary person just enjoys the show.

Grandpas see these movies through a filter. When they perceive values they approve of, they keep thinking: where can we buy a copy of this for the grandchildren?

Psalm 43:3

O send out your light and your truth;
let them lead me; let them bring me to
your holy hill and to your dwelling.

The Lone Oak

When the little granddaughter answers the phone, the man says, "Hi, Honey. This is Grandpa."

She says, matter-of-factly, "Which one?"

For most of the several younger families sprouting from the roots of his family tree, he is the only surviving grandfather. He tends to think of himself in this role, occasionally forgetting for the moment that some of the grandchildren do have another grandfather.

It is quite a responsibility to be the only grandfather.

Titus 2:2

Tell the older men to be temperate, serious, prudent, and sound in faith, in love, and in endurance.

Being There

Closely knit families not long ago could be almost suffocating, with command appearances for dinner every Sunday at Grandpa and Grandma's house.

Now the grandparents have moved to the Sunbelt. The extended family is lucky to get together twice a year.

Even a sophisticated magazine like the *New Yorker* worries about such separations and asks, "How can you be there for each other when you're thousands of miles apart?"

Psalm 79:13

Then we your people, the flock of your pasture, will give thanks to you forever; from generation to generation we will recount your praise.

Games That Zap

Kids tend to think of life as a video game, not realizing that consequences are real.

They shoplift, not really to steal, but on a dare. Zap, they're in serious trouble with police.

They smoke to look cool or merely to rebel. Zap, lung cancer or emphysema.

They experiment with alcohol. Zap, they're dead, either from a traffic crash or a fatal overdose.

Isaiah 32:17

The effect of righteousness will be peace, and the result of righteousness, quietness and trust forever.

Birds of Passage

Autumn sun, low in the sky, peers under the edge of the forest canopy.

It slants a golden spotlight on migrating fall warblers, flitting from thicket to thicket.

Feathers of red and yellow flicker for a moment of bright beauty.

The birds are like grandchildren.

The next time you see them, their plumage will be different.

Matthew 6:29

"Even Solomon in all his glory was not clothed like one of these."

Life Cum Laude

Over the years, colleges have become more vocational than purists would like. But, considering the expense, students can't be blamed for choosing accounting or engineering when a bright medieval history major is still working as a waitress while she looks for a job she can do sitting down.

One grandpa hopes the college kids are furnishing their minds as well as their dorm rooms. In later life, they'll have interesting things to think about—not just to do—when the time for doing has passed.

Proverbs 18:15

An intelligent mind acquires knowledge, and the ear of the wise seeks knowledge.

Electric Shock Therapy

When the chief of the large electrical utility that serves the Chicago area retired suddenly, the newspapers said one of the main reasons was his new grandchild. He realized that in the previous eighteen months he had had time to see the child for only "about ten minutes."

John 6:27

"Do not work for the food that perishes, but for the food that endures for eternal life, which the Son of Man will give you. For it is on him that God the Father has set his seal."

True Art

Some of my artistic friends who have reached grandparent age while enjoying only modest success in their careers are, I sense, a bit disappointed that they haven't achieved more in a lifetime of effort.

They could take consolation from Vincent Van Gogh. Although he was a great artist, he was profoundly unhappy, because his intelligence and spirituality could not cope with his mental illness.

He wrote to his brother: "You are kind to painters, and I tell you the more I think, the more I feel that there is nothing more artistic than to love people."

Acts 17:29

Since we are God's offspring, we ought not to think that the deity is like gold, or silver, or stone, an image formed by the art and imagination of mortals.

Orange and Black

When her mother died, her grandfather tried to comfort her. "I'll take care of you," he said. "I'll never leave you." A few months later, she was wearing an orange and black Halloween costume when they told her Grandpa was dead.

Even after she grew up, on certain bad days, the sight of black and orange together could make her nauseous.

But Grandpa had done all that was truly in his power. He had kept up his life insurance and written a good will.

Psalm 89:48

Who can live and never see death?

Ultimate Trick or Treat

Halloween has become a much more important holiday in recent years than it was when grandfathers were young. We soaped a few windows, bobbed for apples and that was about that.

Promotion of the holiday by the candy and costume industry is one reason. Society in general may be influenced by the Mexican observance of the Day of the Dead. Also, the new focus on Halloween may be related somehow to a growing willingness to talk about death.

That's a subject grandpas need to consider with increasing seriousness even as trick-or-treaters dressed as skeletons are ringing our doorbells.

John 11:25

Jesus said to her, "I am the resurrection and the life. Those who believe in me, even though they die, will live."

Toys for the Rich

As a respected physicist, Freeman J. Tyson is no enemy of technology. But he notes a difference between the advances of earlier times and now.

Technologies like electric light, telephones, refrigerators, radios, TVs, antibiotics and vaccines have truly improved the lives of most people and narrowed the gap between rich and poor.

Now he sees applied science concentrating on "toys for the rich"—developing advanced features for such devices as laptop computers and cellular telephones. Technology, he argues, is most worthwhile when it's "useful, cheap and available to all."

This thought is furnished as a conversation-starter with your granddaughter, the engineering student.

Psalm 41:1

Happy are those who consider the poor; the LORD delivers them in the day of trouble.

Call Waiting

Richard C. Notebaert, chairman of Ameritech, the giant telecommunications company, sat down to write his statement to stockholders for the annual report.

He wanted to make a point about the importance of communications in the modern world. Here's his first sentence: "My first grandchild was born in November—and the first thing he did was try to communicate."

You can tell what was on the top of Notebaert's mind, along with the fortunes of his sixteen-billion-dollar company.

There's a kid who already has grandpa's number.

Psalm 49:1

Hear this, all you peoples; give ear, all inhabitants of the world.

Frequent Flyer Points

Amid the conflicting schedules of parents' night and games at different schools for older siblings, one four-year-old granddaughter needs a place to be for a couple of hours.

Maybe we will sit on a throw rug that's really a flying carpet (it works only so long as you keep your eyes closed) and soar over the house tops to an undiscovered tropical island.

There we will play Parcheesi and eat taffy apples until friendly dragons come to escort her home to bed.

---

1 John 4:8
God is love.

Comedy Tonight

Beware the toy with a suction cup on the end. Sooner or later, it occurs to the adult male to affix the suction cup to his own forehead.

A baby of high chair age invariably finds this excruciatingly funny. Laughter from an audience inspires all standup comics to greater efforts. Unfortunately, a suction cup applied to the forehead ruptures tiny capillaries in the skin and creates a bruise that lasts for a week or more.

So when you see a man on the street with a perfectly round bruise about an inch and half in diameter in the center of his forehead, you know that there was no grandfather in the vicinity to prevent an ill-advised improvisation.

(Don't ask how grandfathers know such things.)

Psalm 91:5

You will not fear the terror of the night, or the arrow that flies by day.

The Patriarch

Grandpa is an old-fashioned type: reliable, industrious, practical.

His new son-in-law is not a bad step-father for the grandchildren, but he's somewhat unstable and unpredictable. He gets more than his share of speeding tickets. He's always upsetting the routines and schedules that would help a family with children operate more smoothly, which leads to more than a little dissension.

Grandpa worries how his grandchildren will turn out. Fortunately, family life experts are saying that a stable grandfather can help keep grandchildren from repeating dysfunctional behavior they see in their own nuclear families. Just by being himself, Grandpa provides an alternative role model.

Psalm 101:2

I will study the way that is blameless. When shall I attain it? I will walk with integrity of heart within my house.

Whose Rules?

It happens sometimes for various reasons that grandparents share the care of their grandchildren with a parent or parents. The kids may very well receive different messages about values and discipline from authority figures of different generations.

This could be a problem if Grandpa believes in the efficacy of willow switches or Mom deals drugs, but generally the differences are about matters like how much allowance is reasonable, which transgressions are serious enough to warrant loss of dessert and what time to go to bed.

None of these differences are serious, family experts agree, as long as the children are guided in the same basic direction.

Romans 15:5

May the God of steadfastness and encouragement grant you to live in harmony with one another, in accordance with Christ Jesus.

Song Without Words

An old friend writes that the years past eighty have made his balance uncertain without a cane. His energy is fading, and his hearing too.

He encloses a snapshot of himself with his two-and-half-year-old granddaughter snuggled in his lap.

There's no failure to communicate here.

———————————————

Psalm 51:8

Let me hear joy and gladness; let the bones that you have crushed rejoice.

Package Label

This carton contains one Perfect Grandchild. Obeys parents. Good manners. Writes "thank you" notes. Always does homework. Mows grass, rakes leaves, shovels snow and takes out garbage without being asked.

Warning: Perfect Grandchild is also perfectly honest. Can't be stopped from pointing out that Grandpa is not a Perfect Grandpa. Cannot be returned to store.

Psalm 25:9

He leads the humble in what is right,
and teaches the humble his way.

Lone Ranger

When you're with your grandchildren and their parents, you can't help wanting to talk part of the time to the adults who are, after all, your own dear children.

But the grandchildren may resent having to share your attention.

Make it up to them by taking them off on an interesting expedition alone with you.

---

2 Corinthians 9:8

And God is able to provide you with every blessing in abundance, so that by always having enough of everything, you may share abundantly in every good work.

There's Worse Advice

Years ago, a young professor volunteered to serve as social secretary and chauffeur for Aldous Huxley during the latter's semester as a visiting professor at the Massachusetts Institute of Technology. The noted British writer was invited to speak all over New England.

En route to one lecture, Huxley confided to his driver: "It's rather embarrassing to have spent one's entire lifetime pondering the human condition and to come toward its close and find that I really don't have anything more profound to pass on by way of advice than, 'Try to be a little kinder.'"

Ephesians 4:32

And be kind to one another, tender-hearted, forgiving one another, as God in Christ has forgiven you.

Unfamiliar Faces

Billy Graham tells in his autobiography that his career as a world-famous evangelist entailed considerable cost to his family life. He writes of returning from his travels and failing to recognize his own offspring: "'Whose baby is this?' I asked, when I saw the child in the arms of a relative."

This is an age of family detachment—emotional and geographic. It's sad to think how many grandfathers could not pick their own grandchildren out of the crowd in a classroom.

Ezekiel 20:18

I said to their children in the wilderness, "Do not follow the statutes of your parents, nor observe their ordinances, nor defile yourselves with their idols."

Compound Interest

Today's grandparents who happen to have a sprightly pack of grandchildren of various ages to gladden their hearts don't fully realize their good fortune.

If the world's current rate of population increase (1.6 percent per year) had held steady since the end of the last Ice Age, the descendants of a single couple would already total a number expressed by fifty-three followed by eighty-two zeroes. So many human bodies would greatly exceed the total amount of matter believed to exist in the universe.

At some point in the future—nobody yet knows exactly how or when—grandchildren will be scarcer than now. That's just plain mathematics.

Revelation 7:9

> *There was a great multitude that no one could count, from every nation, from all tribes and peoples and languages, standing before the throne and before the Lamb, robed in white, with palm branches in their hands.*

Rainy Days

A wise grandpa is someone who remembers that when little kids get in trouble they often have no idea why the grownups are so upset.

To a child, it may seem like such a good idea at the time to cut a design with scissors in the nap blanket or make a slurry of water and detergent on the basement floor to slide on.

Then adult anger comes down like hail from the sky, something that happens for no reason.

Fortunately, grandfatherly mercy can also droppeth as the gentle rain from heaven.

Psalm 37:8

*Refrain from anger, and forsake wrath.
Do not fret—it leads only to evil.*

The Omnivore

While savoring a particularly sweet and succulent squash from the home garden, I brooded about the plight of a granddaughter's school friend. The friend's father makes his daughter eat everything on her plate—a fixation I thought modern parents long ago abandoned.

I remember how much I detested squash as a child. And all other yellow vegetables. And vegetables of all other colors. But I grew up without succumbing to scurvy and found my own way to enjoying all the fruits of the earth. (Well, almost all. I do still draw the line at liver and other entrails.)

In the food war between kids and grownups, I now side with the kids. It's the least a grandpa can do.

Luke 12:23

"For life is more than food, and the body more than clothing."

Pay Per View

TV's Jane Pauley doesn't yet have any grand-children, but she prepared to be a grandmother by taking golf lessons. She told reporters:

"When I'm a grandmother and all I've got is the videotapes (of her old shows) in boxes that the children and grandchildren do not want to watch, what will I do that will make me interesting to them and to myself? Golf is something your children will do with you, because they'll take you...if you pay."

Jeremiah 46:3

Prepare buckler and shield, and advance for battle!

Justice

One of the burdens of educators is the tendency of parents to be defensive. They say their Susie would never pinch a classmate. Or if Mikey isn't learning math, it's the teacher's fault—not that Mikey doesn't do his homework.

But as grandpas know from experience, there are times when teachers, coaches and others in a position to make a child's life miserable do so unfairly.

Then it's time for the family to rally round. If nothing can be done about the person in authority, the small victim can at least be comforted and sustained.

Isaiah 56:1

Thus says the LORD: Maintain justice, and do what is right, for soon my salvation will come, and my deliverance be revealed.

Anam Cara

There's a friend whom I've met for lunch every few weeks for at least forty years. When he walked into the restaurant recently, he projected an unfamiliar sense of urgency.

It turned out that one of his neighbors had died suddenly. I realized that, reminded of the brevity of life at grandfather age, he wanted to reassure himself that I looked healthy. (I did.)

Under his usual crusty exterior I glimpsed what the early Celts called an *anam cara,* Gaelic for "soul friend." Such friends are discovered and recognized, not made.

Sirach 25:9

Happy is the one who finds a friend.

Burrs

Grandpas hug younger grandchildren this time of year at risk of being stabbed by burrs. Likely as not, the kids have been playing in a field or vacant lot where burrs abound.

When grandchildren grow older, the exterior prickles may become psychological. But under the invisible burrs they're still the same kids.

It's too bad that sometimes the psychological prickles repel grandparents, who should know better.

James 3:18

And a harvest of righteousness is sown in peace for those who make peace.

Grandfather's House

"Over the river and through the woods, to Grandmother's house we go...."

That's the way people tend to sing the old song. It makes sense. Grandma probably is the one who supervises putting the turkey in the oven and bakes the pumpkin pies.

But in the official lyrics it's *grandfather's* house that lies over the river and through the woods.

It seems to me that we old coots got more respect in olden times. Maybe today's old coots could be doing something more to earn it.

Lamentations 5:1, 12

Remember, O LORD, what has befallen us; look, and see our disgrace! ...
Princes are hung up by their hands; no respect is shown to the elders.

Thanksgiving

From the viewpoint of grandchildren, Thanksgiving does lack something as a holiday: nobody gets any presents.

But kids do enjoy the other aspects of the day, the feasting and festivity and the chance to play (or perhaps tussle) with cousins.

For adults the lack of presents is a welcome freedom from distraction. In America, Thanksgiving has become an ecumenical holy day. Most religious traditions understand the idea of a communal feast, at which food is shared in the spirit of love.

That's what the day is for.

Psalm 92:1

It is good to give thanks to the LORD, to sing praises to your name, O Most High.

Example

There's a legend retold by Leo Tolstoy, among others. An old grandfather has grown so feeble that he seems a burden to his son and daughter-in-law. One day he drops and breaks the cup he uses for a dish. Annoyed, his daughter-in-law says that from now on she will bring his dinner in the dishpan.

The little grandson is playing on the floor with blocks. The father asks, "What are you making, Misha?" The little boy explains he is making a dishpan, "to feed you and dear Mother when you are old."

Thereafter, the couple wait on the old man with as much care as anyone could wish.

John 13:15

For I have set you an example, that you also should do as I have done to you.

Computation

Grandparents and parents are rightly proud when the grandchildren bring home an "A" in math.

But do we look ahead twenty or thirty years and wonder how that facility with figures will be used?

Grandpas fervently hope it won't be to fiddle with escrow accounts and divert funds from elderly widows.

Researchers say children begin picking up their moral sense even before they can talk, from watching what goes on around them.

Matthew 18:6

"If any of you put a stumbling block before one of these little ones who believe in me, it would be better for you if a great millstone were fastened around your neck and you were drowned in the depth of the sea."

Life among the Yuppi

A museum exhibit contrasts a Hopi pueblo designed for extended families with a modern apartment building, which holds nuclear families who may not even know each other, except to nod in passing.

Sometimes, especially in older "ethnic" neighborhoods, grandparents still occupy the ground floor of a two-flat with the younger generation upstairs. But in individualistic American society this arrangement has come to be viewed as providing perhaps too much closeness.

Still, the experts say children—whether Hopi or Yuppi—can benefit from spending time with their grandfathers.

Psalm 127:1

Unless the LORD builds the house, those who build it labor in vain. Unless the LORD guards the city, the guard keeps watch in vain.

Presence

Missionaries have begun to talk about the "ministry of presence."

The idea is that the mere presence of concerned and sympathetic people somehow does good, whether or not it leads immediately to some more specific kind of service.

Without having heard the phrase, grandfathers have always performed a ministry of presence by showing up at baptisms, birthday parties, recitals and graduations.

Psalm 52:9

I will thank you forever, because of what you have done. In the presence of the faithful I will proclaim your name, for it is good.

Not So Grand

Before the end of this book, something needs to be said about those grandfathers who scarcely serve as role models.

Boring Grandpa has forgotten that children have different interests than adults and need something to do when they come to visit. Grumpy Grandpa can't stand the normal noise of children and doesn't want them around. Bossy Grandpa can't give over telling his grown children and their children how to live their lives. Competitive Grandpa bad-mouths the other grandfather. Nasty Grandpa goes out of his way to criticize everyone destructively and stir up hard feelings throughout the family.

Child psychologists could compile a considerable list of men who needn't apply to be Grandpa of the Year.

Job 21:7

Why do the wicked live on, reach old age, and grow mighty in power?

Even Less Grand

One grandfather, who resented having the grandchildren around during hard times, dumped sharp-edged cinders in his backyard so they would play somewhere else. If they brought home a stray dog or cat, he would kill it.

When their mother was able to take the children and move away, none of them ever looked back.

Psalm 71:4

Rescue me, O my God, from the hand of the wicked, from the grasp of the unjust and cruel.

Memo to Tomorrow

The history teacher suggests that the children make personal time capsules to be opened in ten years.

"Dear Grandchild: I welcome the chance to write these words now because I may not be here in ten years to congratulate you in person on your achievements and bright prospects. But you don't have to do anything more to earn my approval. I admire you just the way you are today. As your future unfolds, you will always know that your grandfather loved you, just as I have basked all my life in the remembered approval of the relatives I knew: my great-grandmother, my grandparents and my parents."

Genesis 9:12-13

God said, "This is the sign of the covenant that I make between me and you and every living creature that is with you, for all future generations: I have set my bow in the clouds, and it shall be a sign of the covenant between me and the earth."

Health Tips from a Vet

Grandfathers remember when it wasn't a virtue to "get in someone's face." So many main characters in books (and movies) now are so nasty one hopes to see them run over by a bus and dispensed with no later than Chapter Two.

A recent biography of James Alfred Wight (pen name "James Herriot") theorizes that this helps explain the immense popularity in the U.S. and Britain of his books and the films based on them.

All Creatures Great and Small and other books in the same vein tell stories derived from the experiences of a country veterinarian in Yorkshire. Their "outdated values—gentleness and kindness" appeal to readers who are sick of a sick culture.

Matthew 11:29

"Take my yoke upon you, and learn from me; for I am gentle and humble in heart, and you will find rest for your souls."

Mourning in America

Grandfathers find themselves riding in funeral processions with increasing frequency. In historical dramas on TV, mourners are often depicted walking with slow dignity to the village churchyard. In modern urban America, mourners' cars roar down the expressway. Drivers have to keep the hearse in sight while dodging the cars cutting in to reach the next exit. This creates considerable risk of being the guest of honor yourself at the next funeral.

When a funeral director from Midland, Michigan, wrote a prize-winning book about his "dismal trade," he pointed out that funerals are more for the living than the dead. We need to recapture rituals that comfort the bereaved and offer hope to all. He writes, "Where death means nothing, life is meaningless."

Matthew 5:4
> *"Blessed are those who mourn, for they will be comforted."*

Catharsis

From the beginning of story-telling, people have identified with the emotions of the main characters. In the end, people feel refreshed and purified even if a story has a sad ending. Talking about this catharsis, Oliver Stone, a successful film director, said audiences can "feel good" after watching a movie hero kill terrorists but it's not a good kind of "feel good." He called it "a kick-ass good feeling."

More subtlety not only makes for better art. It's healthier for the spirit.

Psalm 72:13-14

He has pity on the weak and the needy, and saves the lives of the needy. From oppression and violence he redeems their life; and precious is their blood in his sight.

Check This Out

The checkout line in a supermarket reveals a lot about relationships between children and adults. Sometimes young children seem out of control, as if no one ever reins them in.

Today, it is a father who delivers a continuous monolog: "Stand here...get away from that...I told you to stay with me...do you want me to leave you home next time?"

As near as I can tell, the kids aren't doing anything but fidgeting the way bored children do. I yearn to tell him to shut up and let them be, but it's none of my business.

Ephesians 4:1-2

I therefore, the prisoner in the Lord, beg you to lead a life worthy of the calling to which you have been called, with all humility and gentleness, with patience, bearing with one another in love.

First Snow

Without winter, how would we know about the cycle of life?

There's a time to live, a time to die.

A time to mediate between your children and your grandchildren, and a time to shut your mouth.

Spring will come again, as it always does.

Psalm 104:19

You have made the moon to mark the seasons; the sun knows its time for setting.

Winter Hike

The sun scatters sequins on the snow. Each sparkle speaks of adventure around the bend.

But as the trail of footprints lengthens, the sun lowers in the sky.

The grandchildren skip ahead, but one hiker's steps grow slower.

It seems a long way back to the car.

Still, the woods are no less beautiful than before.

Psalm 27:4

One thing I ask the LORD, that I will seek after: to live in the house of the LORD all the days of my life, to behold the beauty of the LORD, and to inquire in his temple.

Christmas Note

He feels boring. He could almost write the same note as last year.

No tales of hopping on a jet to Majorca. No sky-diving. No wreaking havoc among competitors in business.

Still, sitting over tea with the grandmother, the grandfather reflects that it was a good year for his entire clan.

Nobody lost a job. The trouble about a grandchild's school was resolved. A little one stopped biting.

Yes, a good year.

---

1 Chronicles 16:34

O give thanks to the LORD, for he is good; for his steadfast love endures forever.

Sad News

It doesn't seem so many years since Christmas card notes from friends, young as we were then, told of their new babies, new jobs and other joyful news.

There's still good news this time of year about new grandchildren and well-planned retirements.

But all too often the mail tells of those friends who have left us for the arms of the Lord.

Psalm 56:13

For you have delivered my soul from death, and my feet from falling, so that I may walk before God in the light of life.

Winter Solstice

The shortest day of the year comes soon.

Ancient tribes thought they had to do something to persuade the sun to come back. Led by the grandfathers, they made rattles, beat on drums and danced to the rhythm.

They didn't know that to reach the sun their noise would have to carry six-hundred million miles into space. Still, they felt Someone out there cared about their fears and, to get that Someone's attention, they should do what they could for themselves.

Were they wrong to dance?

Psalm 61:2

From the end of the earth I call to you, when my heart is faint. Lead me to the rock that is higher than I.

How Far, O Lord?

It's useful to keep a journal, even sporadically.

With a journal, a grandpa can recall accurately how long it takes to drive to his grandchildren's favorite sledding hill, with a note about the tricky route to follow after turning left at the old schoolhouse.

He can look back and see how much he weighed on this day last year. At holiday feasting time, that's good to know in advance.

A journal that also records his thoughts can help him judge whether the passing of a year has brought him closer to being a better person.

Luke 6:49

"But the one who hears and does not act is like a man who built a house on the ground without a foundation. When the river burst against it, immediately it fell, and great was the ruin of that house."

No Ice Breaker

Two boys walk across the frozen surface of a pond in the woods. If the ice cracks under them, mounting a rescue effort here would be a considerable problem. I should shout at them to get off the ice. But they probably would respond only with a rude gesture.

Fortunately, while I watch, nervously looking around for a long pole that might be useful if needed to pull them out, they finish their crossing safely.

In a smaller community, I would know those boys and they would know me. I would merely have to threaten to tell their grandfather what they were doing and they'd stop.

Psalm 69:15

> *Do not let the flood sweep over me, or the deep swallow me up.*

Tooth and Consequences

The phone rings. The young caller proudly announces the loss of another tooth. The grandfather proclaims his awe at the courage of the tooth-loser.

Grandpa would be equally willing to admire the beauty of the tooth itself, but it has vanished in the night to be replaced by a sum of money under the pillow. So he rejoices instead in the young person's mysterious new-found wealth.

This is just one of the reasons God created grandfathers.

Ephesians 4:1-2

I therefore, the prisoner in the Lord, beg you to lead a life worthy of the calling to which you have been called, with all humility and gentleness, with patience, bearing with one another in love.

Quiet Please

Compared to most grandmothers, most grandfathers seem a bit remote. Most of us can carry on a respectable conversation, but we seem to lack the gene for chewing over family events in sufficient detail to satisfy our female relatives.

However, grandchildren want to be listened to. *That* grandpas can do, truly focusing on what the kids have to say and conveying that we consider them and their concerns truly important.

Isaiah 42:18

Listen, you that are deaf; and you that are blind, look up and see!

Wrapping Up Symbols

Christmas shopping is complicated because gifts are meaningful symbols as well as things. Here's an example:

When a college professor lectured on Thoreau's famous disdain for personal possessions, he noticed that one student seemed troubled. Speaking to her after class, he learned that she felt guilty because she valued her clothes and furniture so highly.

When her parents escaped from North Korea, robbers took everything but the clothes her parents were wearing. The girl's possessions weren't just comforts; they were reminders of all that her parents had suffered and the modest gains from hard work that year by year had enabled her family to build a new life in a new country.

Exodus 23:9

You shall not oppress a resident alien; you know the heart of an alien, for you were aliens in the land of Egypt.

Sorrow and Sunshine

Friends report that one of their grandchildren has been found to have a serious chronic health problem. They now have a worry that, like the rims of their glasses, lurks always at the edge of their vision.

The more children and grandchildren there are, the more vulnerable a family is to the tribulations of life: accidents, diseases, heartbreak and other disappointments and disasters.

To be free for a time of any such serious worries is a golden moment for which a grandpa should give thanks.

Romans 7:25

Thanks be to God through Jesus Christ our Lord!

Security

One winter morning, a child broke through the ice on the Des Plaines River. Responding to her screams, the mother fell through the ice herself. Both drowned.

A reporter arrived in time to see a gray-haired man drive up in an old car. "Get in," he said to the remaining children. As they started to obey, the police intervened. They didn't know who the old man was.

It turned out that he was the dead woman's father. She hadn't got along with him when she was alive, but in the end the grandfather proved to be the only security the surviving children had.

Psalm 44:26

*Rise up, come to our help. Redeem us
for the sake of your steadfast love.*

Mirror, Mirror on the Wall

Despite all the recent gains for women in American society, researchers report continuing angst among girls of junior high age. From about age nine to fourteen, their self-esteem declines. Girls fret about their appearance and popularity.

Although young boys of the same ages are gaining control of their environment through greater size and strength, they too can benefit from seeing themselves through grandpa's approving eyes.

Grandfathers can't solve all the problems of growing grandchildren, but we can remain an unfailing source of encouragement and affection.

Psalm 17:7

Wondrously show your steadfast love,
O savior of those who seek refuge from
their adversaries at your right hand.

Vision

The grandpa complains during his periodic eye check-up that even with his reading glasses on, he has trouble reading small type.

There isn't much that can be done. The problem, the doctor says, is "maturity." The man's eyesight isn't bad, considering his age. The doctor gives him a new and slightly different eyeglass prescription but says not to fill it unless he loses or breaks his present glasses.

The man comes away curiously cheered. He can still see what's in front of him. And he could never see into the future anyway.

Ecclesiastes 10:14

No one knows what is to happen, and who can tell anyone what the future holds?

Hi to "High Touch"

The business gurus who charge three hundred dollars a ticket for their seminars are still talking about the importance of "high touch" in an age of high technology.

(Some businesses still don't get the idea. If you phone in with a mild complaint, by the time you have gone a few rounds with their automatic voice mail you are pondering the possibilities of a class-action lawsuit.)

For grandparents, high touch means interacting as persons with grandchildren, not just sending them the latest video games for Christmas.

Genesis 27:21

Then Isaac said to Jacob, "Come near, that I may feel you, my son, to know whether you are really my son Esau or not."

Best Sellers

A prominent literary critic recently observed that the most popular subjects for books have scarcely changed since before printing was even invented.

Five centuries ago, when books were written out laboriously by hand, they were mostly about religion, animals, how-to, travel or cookery—still the best-selling categories.

Underneath the strange haircuts, grandchildren have the same interests, feelings and fears, not only as ourselves at their ages, but also as our ancestors.

Psalm 22:4

In you our ancestors trusted; they trusted, and you delivered them.

Naughty Children

People once thought children inherently tended to evil and the Devil had to be beaten out of them.

At certain bad moments, when children are behaving more outrageously than usual, one can see where that idea came from.

The truth is more prosaic: none of us is perfect. Not children, not parents, not grandparents. We should all try harder to be better.

Meanwhile, it's a good idea to interfere when the children start attacking their siblings with blunt instruments.

Romans 12:2

Do not be conformed to this world, but be transformed by the renewing of your minds, so that you may discern what is the will of God—what is good and acceptable and perfect.

Ode to Joy

Having just learned to write, she has already composed a poem.

The gist of it seems to be that she thinks it's fun to come to Grandpa and Grandma's house.

Who needs Whitman or Longfellow...or even Bob Dylan?

Psalm 81:2

*Raise a song, sound the tambourine,
the sweet lyre with the harp.*

Signs and Wonders

A skilled magician refuses to perform in front of little children. He says when they're that young they assume grown-ups can do anything.

Children's assumption of adult omnipotence is a mixed blessing for grandpas. When children come with a broken toy, it's great to be Grandpa the Wonderworker who fixes it. Not so great is having to explain that the job is hopeless.

---

2 Corinthians 13:7

> *But we pray to God that you may not do anything wrong—not that we may appear to have met the test, but that you may do what is right, though we may seem to have failed.*

Story Tellers

When I checked my public library for the subject, "grandfathers," the computer turned up more than 300 listings. Most of them were stories.

William Elliott Hazelgrove, a rising young novelist, tells of being inspired by both of his grandfathers, both irrepressible story-tellers. One of them kept a scrapbook. After a first novel that made little impression on the literary world, Hazelgrove mined the scrapbook for material and wrote a second novel that was widely acclaimed, republished abroad and made into a movie.

If one of your grandchildren grows up to be a writer, one way or another you'll be put in a book.

Psalm 78:4

We will tell to the coming generation the glorious deeds of the LORD, and his might, and the wonders that he has done.

Lessons

When Grandpa came to visit for the weekend, the first grandchild up on Sunday morning would find the old man already in the kitchen, waiting for someone to save his knees by bringing him a can of beer from the refrigerator.

Years later, grown-up grandchildren remembered taking him and his numerous eccentricities as much for granted as that refrigerator. "He played Steal the Bundle and other card games with us by the hour," they said. "He was fun."

There were etiquette lessons, too, such as the rule in Poker against picking up cards before everyone's hand has been dealt. Everything grandfathers do and say in the presence of grandchildren teaches them something.

Proverbs 8:10

Take my instruction instead of silver,
and knowledge rather than choice gold.

Real Cool

When the little boy fell into the river, his mother was only inches away. She immediately grabbed the scruff of his shirt with a grip that would have shamed a pitbull.

Leaping to lend unneeded help, the father tripped on a loose rock and sprained his ankle. The problem now wasn't the wet little boy, already warmly wrapped. It was getting the injured father to a car.

Fortunately, the grandfather was already bringing the car to the victim instead of vice versa. A retired firefighter, Grandpa had some experience in such things. The little boy learned a lot that day.

Sirach 40:24

Kindred and helpers are for a time of trouble.

Gifts

Only in the ads are diamonds forever.

After the excitement of Christmas passes, the gifts lose their glitter. The little ones' bright new toys begin to break or run out of batteries. The check signed by grandpa for grandchildren old enough to be saving up for something will be cashed and the money soon spent.

The gift that will last in grandchildren's hearts will be the hours grandpa spends with them throughout the year.

Psalm 19:10

More to be desired are they than gold, even much fine gold; sweeter also than honey, and drippings of the honey-comb.

Christmases Past

Although Christmas in America has become a melange of pagan winter festival and shopping frenzy, the spiritual significance has not been entirely lost.

Children prepare for Christmas in an agony of anticipation over the presents they hope for. But in later years their warm memories of Christmas revolve around the love they experienced from parents and grandparents. Most of the gifts they don't even remember.

People who never experienced such a Christmas are the ones for whom the holiday season brings not joy but depression.

In time, the excesses of Christmas drop away like the dry needles from the Christmas trees, allowing the love that warms the world to shine forth.

Luke 2:10

> But the angel said to them, "Do not be afraid; for see—I am bringing you good news of great joy for all the people."

Pumped Up

Home video:

SCENE 1. A little girl is getting a sidewalk bike passed along from an older cousin. We see the bike coming off the car roof. We see the little girl jumping up and down with excitement and hear her squeals.

SCENE 2. Close up. We see her disappointment when it's discovered that the tires, not having been used in a while, have lost their air.

SCENE 3. We see the grandfather go to his car and pull out an electric tire pump that runs off the cigaret lighter. He pumps up the tires.

SCENE 4. The little girl wobbles off down the sidewalk on the bike with an expression of pure joy. Pan to the grandfather. His expression suggests he thinks, for the moment, that this is the reason he was born.

Psalm 34:17

*When the righteous cry for help, the
LORD hears, and rescues them from all
their troubles.*

A Monkey on His Back

The monkey kept trying to kill the turtle in various ways. When the monkey hurled down thorns from the treetop, the turtle pulled into its shell. Pushed into a river to drown, the turtle merely swam away.

A talented California eighth-grader won a writing contest with an account of how much she enjoyed the stories told by her grandfather from the Philippines. Only after he grew weaker and died did she realize that her grandfather's stories of the monkey and the turtle were really telling her about himself. He was at first the turtle, postponing death, but in the end he was the monkey, unable to rid himself of cancer.

Psalm 116:3-4

The snares of death encompassed me; the pangs of Sheol laid hold on me; I suffered distress and anguish. Then I called on the name of the LORD: "O LORD, I pray, save my life!"

Business as Usual

Parts of the Bible seem surprisingly modern. One episode that has always impressed me is the uproar among the silversmiths when St. Paul went to Ephesus.

They were cashing in on local worship of the goddess Artemis (Diana) by selling silver religious momentoes to tourists. They were angry because they feared Paul's teaching might be bad for business.

At least these merchants were honest about their motives. Today, people seem quick to declare they are standing up for free enterprise or welfare reform or whatever when what really concerns them is what would be bad—or good—for their own selfish interests.

Psalm 49:17

For when they die they will carry nothing away; their wealth will not go down after them.

Light Load

Holiday family hike.

The littlest one begins to lag behind, asking to be carried. She's heavy, padded like a polar bear cub, with bulky boots. The adults take turns as beasts of burden: Mommy, Daddy and Grandpa.

Grandpa is pleased still to be useful in such a basic way.

Matthew 11:30

"For my yoke is easy, and my burden is light."

Sunsets

"Red sky at night, sailors delight.

Red sky in morning, sailors take warning."

That's the kind of good advice grandfathers are supposed to know about. But if you get turned around, and can't tell east from west, a sunset doesn't look different from a sunrise.

Grandfathers are closer to sunset than to sunrise. That's OK. Maybe we've done enough doing. Now is the time for just being. And enjoying sunsets.

Ecclesiastes 1:14

I have seen all things that are done under the sun, and behold, all is vanity and a chase after the wind.

New Year's Eve

A year is like a life. As it draws to an end, the time to do things differently runs out.

Psalm 34:22

The LORD redeems the life of his servants; none of those who take refuge in him will be condemned.